IN-TRANSIT
The Story of a Journey

IN-TRANSIT
The Story of a Journey

Sadie Vernon

Edited by Judy Lumb

Producciones de la Hamaca, 2019

Copyright 2000 Sadie Vernon

Cover Art by Judy Lumb, Caye Caulker, BELIZE

Published by *Producciones de la Hamaca*, Caye Caulker, BELIZE

Second Edition by *Producciones de la Hamaca*, Caye Caulker, BELIZE.

Paperback ISBN 978-976-8273-09-3

E-book ISBN 978-976-8273-10-9

First Edition Published and Printed in 2000 by The Angelus Press, Belize City, BELIZE, Sixth Publication in their *BELIZE CHRONICLES SERIES*

ISBN 976-8142-16-2

Contents

Foreword from Belize viii
Foreword from the United States x
Preface to the First Edition xii
Acknowledgements xiv
From the Editor xv

Chapter One: Growing Up in Belize (1920-41)
My Childhood 1
The Good Shepherd 11
Big School 12
The 1931 Hurricane 14
High School 16
My Brother Frederick 21
My Father 24
A Living Stream 25

Chapter Two: Jamaica (1941-43)
In Transit in Barbados 29
Kingston—Looking for Work 32
Next to the Wall 37
Carron Hall 43
Along Uncharted Ways 52
Making Connections 61
Appendicitis 64
The Lonely Place 66
A New Friend 68
The Old Servant 73
The Trusting Child 77
Another Transition 78

Chapter Three: Turks and Caicos Islands (1944-1949)
Solitude and Sweet Potatoes 81
A Baby Saved 82
Twins 82
A Vision and a Dream 86
A Trip to North Carolina 87
Being Put Out of the Anglican Church 91
Leaving Turks and Caicos 93

Chapter Four: Highgate (1950-56)
Continuation School 95
A Concert at Highgate 102
A Call for Help 103
A Terrifying Dream 104
Friends Meeting 105
Lyndale 106
Friends Conference in Greensboro 107

Chapter Five: Sojourns in the United States (1957-1960)
Practical Nurse Training 109
Preemies 111
Room 19 113
A Sick Baby 114
Ernestine Calls 115
Night Supervisor 116
Train to Kentucky 123
Brother Charles 125
Carmel Meeting 126
Earlham School of Religion 128
Speaking to Friends in the United States 130
Return to British Honduras 139

Chapter Six: Belize (1960-2008)
From this Valley They Say You Are Going 140
Going Home 141
Christian Social Council 142
Hurricane Hattie 142
Ecumenical Movement 144
Belmopan Hostel 146
Mina Grant Centre 147
Belize Continuation School 147
Community Development in St. Martin de Porres 150
Reconciling Ministries 154
Confronting Violence 155
Attending Death 157
United Church of Christ Support 158
Canning and Sewing Projects 158
Friends Support the Work of the Council 160

Word from Belize 161
Belize Council of Churches 162
State of the Nation 164

Chapter Seven: Space, Time and Eternity
Feelings I Do Not Understand 168
Visions 171
Communication with the Dead 175
Living and Working Alone 176
Living without Fear 177
Obscenities 180
Space, Time and Electricity 183

Appendix: Honours and Awards
Outstanding Citizen Award, St. John's College 187
Personality of the Month, The New Belize 187
Outstanding Volunteer of the Year Award,
   Belize Council of Voluntary Social Services 189
Commander of the Most Excellent Order
   of the British Empire 189
Distinguished Alumnus, Earlham School of Religion   189
Honorary Doctor of Divinity, Earlham School
   of Religion 189
Recorded as a Minister, Western Yearly Meeting 193
Paul Harris Award, Rotary International 193
Public Recognition Ceremony, Belize Council
   of Churches 194
Sadie Vernon High School 195
Introduction of Ms. Sadie Vernon 195
Sadie Vernon High: The Temple of My Learning 196

Foreword from Belize

If publication is a way of gauging the level of a nation's sophistication, then Belize is certainly moving forward, actually taking strides within the past few years. In our bookstores there are now items by Belizeans that are works of literary merit: scholarly works, children's books, dictionaries, etc. Where we are short and need much more to fill the vacuum is in the area of biographies. I say this because there are so many persons, who have contributed in their own way to our collective well-being, and are now gradually passing into the next life without leaving for posterity accounts of their lives.

Miss Sadie—as she is affectionately known—has righted her score with the next generation in putting together this book. Compiling all the information with the help of Judy Lumb was an act of selfless sharing for which Miss Sadie is well known. It did not make any difference whether you were a struggling mother who needed some desperate attention or a lofty member of the Belize Council of Churches, with which she was associated for several years. Her life has been one of giving, consoling, advocating, teaching and generally ministering. We often met during meetings of NGOs and she always made her intervention on the part of her very large extended family of people in need. It is a distinct pleasure to see this being brought out in the book.

The book is small but it is many things. In it I saw an account of experiences by a person who is a missionary; who is regional in covering the Caribbean, the U.S., and Belize; who is a visionary and gifted with a sixth sense of the unknown. Furthermore, it is told by a woman who sees life from the perspective of relationships with family, friends, clients, and the downtrodden. All of these coalesce into chapters that become episodes in the transition.

Miss Sadie and Judy Lumb have done us in Belize and the wider region a tremendous favour. If it stimulates others to come forward and share their story, the success of the favour would ripen even more.

Joseph O. Palacio
January 1998
Resident Tutor, University of the West Indies

Foreword from the United States

Sadie Vernon has touched Friends (Quakers) in the United States in many ways, and we gratefully claim her as our own. She came to us first after her involvement in Jamaica, telling us about the work and the people there. What we remember is her love for God and concern for His children.

In early 1972 my husband, Ercil, and I were guests of Sadie in Belize. She took us to the schools, the places and people served by the Christian Social Council. Through it all we saw a Sadie who ached to see children, young people, and mothers given the opportunity to fulfil their possibilities. She introduced us to leaders in government, and we saw that she was not only recognized and respected, but she was also listened to.

In a pre-Easter service in the Anglican Church one evening Sadie gave the message, the first woman to speak from that pulpit. Her words made it clear from whence came her vision, her guidance, her love.

Following our visit, American Friends, especially Friends Women, became partners with Sadie in her service in Belize. Sadie has come to be with us in conferences and other meetings, spoken passionately of the work being done, and her vision of ways it can be expanded. Her devotional messages and personal conversations have been revelations of the depth of her faith. Her gentle, loving spirit has been Light to us.

This is the Sadie we have known, and we will be grateful for her book that tells us of her early years and experiences, and of her country with which we feel a kindship.

She writes of her "second sight", extra sensory experiences, deep desire to explore new concepts, new ways of thinking, but always "secure with what I know and believe". Her words brought a picture of a tree, the upper limbs blown by the wind in great swings in all directions, but held secure by the lower limbs and trunk rooted deeply in the ground.

That is Sadie. Her questing spirit has the freedom to explore and embrace new ideas, new ways of seeing life and relationship with God and all His creation, because she is rooted in the Eternal.

Maxine Hoover Beane, January, 1998
President (1968-1974)
United Society of Friends Women, International

Preface to the First Edition

Knowing Sadie Vernon and helping her to publish her story has been one of the great joys of my life. Before I moved to Belize in June of 1987, I had heard of Sadie Vernon's work in Belize from a Friends publication. I had intended to look her up, but forgot until my second month in Belize when I heard on the radio news that she had been made a Commander of the British Empire. I wrote her a letter and we soon met.

From the time I first met Miss Sadie, I was in awe of her presence and her position in the community. She invited me to come to the Friday morning worship service for the Girls Continuation School. I attended, but I slipped out quietly at the end, not wanting to be a bother. The next time I saw Miss Sadie, she chided me for disappearing and said I should have stayed to chat with her. From then on, I made it a point to visit her whenever I was in Belize City. I always felt like she could see right through to the heart of me. Reflecting later upon conversations I often found little jewels, profound wisdom that addressed some issue in my life I had not even mentioned.

I was really honoured when she asked me to help publish her autobiography. It is a story of great courage, faith, compassion, and spiritual depth. She tells of her happy childhood in Belize City, her sorrow at the loss of her mother, her adjustment to life in Jamaica, her teaching successes, her nursing experiences in the United States, her ecumenical work with the Belize Council of Churches, and her unusual visions and dreams. Before she gets a vision, Miss Sadie tells us that she first sees swirling colours, which are reflected in the painting on the cover of this book and the graphic at the beginning of each chapter.

Working with her words has been a very fulfilling experience. When she writes of an experience, she does not reflect upon it from the present, but puts herself there, in that time and place. She uses the vocabulary of that time and prefers the King James translation of the Bible, the Bible of her childhood.

When Miss Sadie was growing up, that which is now the country of Belize was British Honduras and the city was referred to as Belize. She introduced herself as being from Belize, British Honduras. In the late 1970s the name of the country was changed to Belize and the city became Belize City. The word "Belize" is used in two ways in this book, in the early years to mean Belize City, and in the later years to mean the country of Belize.

One aspect of Miss Sadie's style of writing may be difficult for some readers. In describing her experiences with race relations in the United States in the 1950s, Miss Sadie uses the word "coloured" to refer to herself and "the blacks" to those who are now called "African-Americans." It was the terminology used at that time and has been maintained here to be consistent with her style of writing. For the same reason, some language is used that would now be considered sexist. To change her words to reflect current vocabulary seemed artificial and, as her editor and with her concurrence, I chose not to violate the integrity of her writing.

Miss Sadie has been important to many lives in many parts of the world, but especially here in Belize and in the United States, so there are two Forewords, one from each country. As she has counselled and inspired many, many people, it is our hope that by publication of her story she will continue to counsel and inspire.

Judy Lumb, Editor
January, 1998
Caye Caulker, Belize

Acknowledgments

Many people have helped to bring this book to fruition. We are grateful to our reviewers and proofreaders, Dr. Joseph Palacio, Maxine Hoover Beane, Florence Emma Peery, Rosemary Stadler, Blanche Morrell, Eva Middleton, Lawrence Vernon, Father Leroy Flowers, Rev. Moises Chan, Mike and Kay Cain, Barbara Harris, and Johan Maurer.

Photographs, letters, and other information were provided by Jean Stewart, Elmer and Maxine Featherston, John Meyers at Friends United Meeting, Earlham School of Religion, and Luis Avila and Kenner Pascascio at the Belize Archives. Thanks to Maxine and Elmer Featherstone for providing transcripts of presentations given at Friends gatherings.

We are especially grateful to Ray Castillo, Jean Shaw and her son, Tommy Shaw, for their hospitality and tender loving care.

And, finally, this book would not have been possible without the steadfast work of Dylan Vernon, Editor, and the financial and technical support of the Angelus Press.

We thank you all!

Sadie Vernon
Judy Lumb
April 15, 2000

From the Editor

Although this is a second edition, the text remains the same because Miss Sadie is no longer with us to approve any changes. She left this world December 1, 2008. I miss her still. I was tempted to involve those who prepared the Kriol dictionary and change Sadie's spellings of language used both in Belize and in Jamaica, but again, she is not here to approve any changes, so none were made.

The first printing was published by The Angeles Press, before on-demand printing was available. Those first copies of the book are now all gone, but there are still people in Belize and in the U. S. who want to read Sadie's story. So *Producciones de la Hamaca* is now re-publishing the same book on-demand so it will be available for the foreseeable future. Some of the photos used in the first edition are no longer available, so others are included in their place. Thanks to Neil Snarr for voluntarily sending that beautiful photo on the next page when I told him I was republishing Sadie's book. Thanks to Tom Hamm and Jenny C. Freed from Friends United Meeting's archives, we have photos to replace those in the first edition. As always, Mary Alpuche was very helpful as she found the photos from the Belize National Archives that we had used in the first edition. Thanks to everyone for your help!

Again, it is my great joy to present Sadie Vernon's story in her own words.

Judy Lumb
Caye Caulker, Belize,
January 18, 2019

Sadie Vernon at Quaker Knoll Camp of Wilmington Yearly Meeting in the 1980s.

CHAPTER ONE
Growing Up in Belize (1920-41)

I often wondered what the teachers thought who wanted to write me off. But what I learned most of all was extremely important—never to write off anyone. In my teacher years, it was really important to me to go all out for those who had been given over to failure. Within the human person there has to be a reachable place, a responsive place, and if we understand that, how many can be saved from the hopeless end to which adults have driven them?

My Childhood

I was born on March 20, 1918, the daughter of Elsa Agatha Maheia Vernon and Frederick Vernon. My mother's family was dominant in my life. Her parents were Sarah Lee Brown and Benjamin Lee Maheia. Mr. Brown, my great-grandfather, had come from Scotland. The Browns were a big family in Belize City. My grandparents had nine children, Annette, Agnes, Lena, Elsa (my mother), Nora, Kathleen, Rosalind, Alfred, Wallace, and Percy. My Aunt Kathleen was my favourite. I had a tender scalp and she would comb my hair very gently.

I had a very happy childhood. My mother, my younger brother, and I lived in Belize City with our Aunt Annette, whom we called "Ga", short for "godmother". It was actually our grandmother's house, but she stayed most of the time in Mullins River. My aunts, Agnes and Rosalind, married and moved out, but my mother married and stayed. Two of my uncles lived in that big family house, too, Wallace and Percy.

My grandfather had built that house for my Granny. He did not just put the supports flat with a nail through, he used a method called "mortis and tenon", where the beams are cut so they fit together. That made the house very strong, so it has always felt safe to me. It went through both the 1931 hurricane and Hurricane Hattie.

My father's father, also named Frederick Vernon, was a mahogany foreman. According to my father, the Vernons were originally from France, three brothers setting out to seek their fortune. One went to Jamaica and two settled on St. George's Caye. On the Caye they were very interested in education and educated their children well. My father had two brothers, Eldred and Edwin, and two sisters, Agatha and one we called "Bebe", who died in childbirth.

My Granny Vernon was a Mutrie. She had two sisters who lived at the cayes and came in now and then. Their father was from France and their mother must have been a Maya Indian because they looked Mayan to us, but we never asked questions like that. The Mutries sounded very funny to us because they were French.

Once there was a party for a new priest and his wife. She was French Canadian and what really tickled my brother and me was her speech. After we were called in to shake hands with them, we went back to the dining room, killing ourselves with laughter. She sounded just like the Mutries.

On Sundays we went to visit Granny Vernon, who was sure to be sitting in the kitchen smoking her pipe. She never had much to say, but we liked to go in her house that had a winding staircase. When my grandfather was alive, he liked to sit at the top of the stairs and look out on the happenings on the street.

CHAPTER ONE: Growing up in Belize

He was very clear-skinned and had a long white beard. When he died, we were not taken to see him nor did we go to the funeral.

My brother was eighteen months younger than I. Just as children of today we did not like rainy days. The old stand-by was hauled out.

"Rain, rain, go away, come again some other day."

He and I spent many hours playing with the neighbourhood children in our big yard. My grandfather said there should only be one big family house on the lot, so we were the only ones with a big yard. Since none of the other houses had a yard, all the children from Albert Street came to play in our yard.

We had one almond tree, four mango trees, one May plum tree, one governor plum tree, so-called because a governor brought it from the east. There was a soursap tree and a kinep tree that took ever so long to bear. That tree really bothered us. We listened to older people talking about trees that took long to produce fruit. We tried driving rusty nails into the main trunk; we pleaded with that tree. Our tree did bear, not much the first time, but after that it really paid us well for our interest and our prayers. To our great sorrow, the tree was uprooted in the 1931 hurricane and that was the end of it. It was a beautiful tree that not many people have, even today. There is a huge one on South Street, not far from where I live, that just will not bear. It is twice the size of the one we had and I hope that when it decides to bear fruit I will get a few kineps from the owner for all my genuine interest in that tree.

I still live in that same house with that same big yard. I still have two mango trees, one of which is a Bombay mango, one small plum tree, a soursap tree, a grapefruit, an acerola cherry tree and one avocado tree (locally called "pear") that will not bear. It is acting like that kinep tree. Every year I talk to it. I threaten it. I am trying to be patient with it, but many people tell me they gave up on theirs and had it cut down. Sometimes

I think about Jesus and that cursed fig tree, but I do not have the courage to curse this pear tree. Maybe this will be its year.

My brother and I did not quarrel much and we shared. One of the best experiences was to have Mama at home when we came from school. She did not have much to give us, but every day she had a surprise in the safe. We never took it from the safe, but she would bring out something wrapped in shop paper. Miss Jessie, who sold Dumps (a peppermint candy) from house to house, always left a piece for each of us. Sometimes we got one biscuit each or a piece of tableta, a grated coconut candy, or cut up brute, a sugar sweet made of coconut candy that was hard to chew.

I was upstart and rude. I gave an eye for an eye, but they seldom punished me, so I thought I could say anything. I had an answer for everything. If they scolded me, I went under the house and stayed until I thought they would not scold me anymore. If Granny were there, no one could shout at us. She did not believe in that. She said you must speak to children quietly.

Under the house I had one of those heavy, grey papers that come around bails. I kept it under the beams of the northwest corner of the house. There it was always dry. That was my reading corner. On Saturdays we were free to do what we wanted in the afternoons. Carrie Smith was my friend. She lived on the north side and would come through the gate so we could sit under the house and talk. At night, she did not have a strict bedtime, so she sat out on her step and I was by the window in my aunt's bed. We talked and talked.

There was a stream where Tigris Street is now, where the boys went to fish. There was only one house on West Street and nothing beyond.

School holidays were in May, during the dry season. There was little water in Belize City. There were long

CHAPTER ONE: Growing up in Belize

lines at the government rainwater tanks in St. John's school yard. People would come and put their buckets in line from 5 a.m. before it opened at 7 o'clock. We had a vat, which never went dry, but we left the city.

All the children, my brother and I with our nine cousins, went to Mullins River where my grandmother lived. In those days there were three large sailboats, called "sandlighters", that carried passengers to Mullins River. One of them is still working, a blue boat called the "Radio". It docks over by the Fort.

The trip took about four hours. There was no water in Mullins River, either, so we would go to Sandy Bay by the river for a whole day. We did the washing and cooked. Then we brought water back in the big half drums to use in Mullins River. We had wonderful times during those vacations.

Food, clothes and shelter were never problems I knew of growing up. There were school clothes, Sunday clothes, school shoes, Sunday shoes and things had to be well cared for. My aunt bought me everything, clothes, shoes—always the latest button-side shoes. She would send a note with me to Mr. Lord at the Biddle's store, which was right next to where the Post Office is now. They put me on a chair to button the shoes and put on the cap for Sunday School. Saturday chores paid a whole shilling, and then a shilling bought a lot.

For us birthdays were very important. Since my birthday is March 20, it was always in Lent. Because of that I could not have a party, but I did get my favourite food—rice and beans and meatballs. As I was not fond of white cake, I asked for bread pudding. I was quite happy with that.

My brother's birthday was Christmas Eve, so he had it all—his favourite food and a party. He invited friends and we played games and afterward had cake, candy, biscuits (the British word for cookies) and lemonade.

In those days, church services were held every morning and all Anglican children went to church on their birthday to receive a special blessing from the priest. Adults were there, too, so all who had the same birthday were there and that was fun. Often the priest had not shaved and his growing hairs felt very funny as he gave his kiss. I wonder if he ever thought of that problem.

Whenever it was your birthday, you got to choose a hymn. I always chose "God Eternal Mighty King." My aunt asked "Why you pick a hymn like that?" They could not understand why I would, as a small child, but that hymn just struck my fancy. There were things in it that meant a lot to me. It has a verse that says,

> *Martyrs in a noble Host,*
> *of the cross are heard to boast*
> *Oh that we our cross may bear*
> *and a crown of glory wear.*

As little children we knew who the martyrs were, those who were killed, had their necks chopped off or were burned at the stake, because we kept those saint days. We learned who St. Luke and Mary Magdalena were, long before we could read about them. We knew about them through hymns. Because of the tunes, we learned to sing the words even though we did not understand all of it. Church was really a learning place.

Church parties and the Christmas Bazars were great events for me because our house was near to the school where things were held. A lot of activity went on at our house and children helped carry things over. A lot of learning went on, too, and it became easy to help with teas and suppers.

I have never been one for planning very far ahead, and I know that in my early years planning often ended in disappointment. My very busy family was involved with church. There were meetings, funerals, unexpected visitors, and we often ended up having plans changed.

CHAPTER ONE: Growing up in Belize

St. John's Cathedral where Ms. Sadie grew up sitting near the organ (*Courtesy Belize National Archives*)

My brother and I played church and knew a lot of hymns by heart. A congregation of one was not enough so we set up chairs and went through it as though many were there.

Church was a very important place for me. Because Ga was the organist. I was fortunate to be able to sit near the organ in the gallery, where I could look through the spokes on all the interesting things below.

The Hulses came through the north door and dear Mrs. Evadne liked hats with flowers. Miss Erica Phillips, later Lady Wolffsohn, used the south door. She looked like a queen; she was beautiful and liked broad hats. Mis Maude Sebastian held my attention as she came in the north door. Miss Ivy Hyde came in the west door, so I could only see her as she came from under the gallery. Lots of people were there every Sunday. The cross-bearer was Mr. Headley Watson and the entry of choir and clergy was always moving. Sometimes they wore red cassocks and sometimes black, but always with white surplices.

The highlight of these processions was the Bishop. His fancy robes fascinated me, especially the sleeves. They were very pretty, big and puffy with a red ribbon around the wrist. Bishop Dunn was tall and full-bodied. The mitre and staff made him a very important figure indeed. Usually after church he would stand at the back door shaking hands and blessing little children by putting his hands around their heads. It felt right. Everyone wore hats so he did not have to worry about getting greasy hands! We thought that was the holiest thing you could experience. We really revered the Bishop, but he was not there every Sunday only now and then.

We children really enjoyed Matins, the regular church service that does not include communion. We listened in for the parts in which we could join. Sunday after Sunday, year in, year out, we learned a great deal by rote. There was also the anticipation of coming events like Advent, when they sang, "Deeply Wailing" and "Alleluia", or Lent when it was "Forty Days and Forty Nights". Easter had "Jesus Christ Is Risen Today". Christmas was the best with all the carols. We went around singing carols to the old and the sick. There was nothing like "Once in Royal David's City."

The Liturgy and the hymns wove themselves into the fibre of my being to be there forever, no matter where I went or what happened in my life. The joy of worship was real and we all struggled early to find the page numbers. Everyone had to have a book, even if it was upside down. The Liturgy was important because it allowed the priest and the people to have separate parts, vesicles and responses. That had great meaning for me.

For Cathedral children the Benedicite gave something that nothing else did. Every verse ends with "Praise Him and magnify Him forever." When all the big people finished singing the first of each verse, all the little children joined in with "Praise Him and magnify Him forever". We waited just for that, so we were ready.

CHAPTER ONE: Growing up in Belize

Years later when flying in aeroplanes I have been glad for that Benedicite because I have found myself praying, "Seas and floods, clouds, thunders and lightning". As I have looked from above at the sea, knowing bounds over which it shall pass, I have spoken to the winds and the clouds with a oneness learned from the Benedicite. In quiet and stormy times, knowing all the works of the Lord, what more can one do than "praise Him and magnify Him forever". I have felt a very strong oneness at these times, my oneness with all things. I have been in places that were full of disquiet—storms, raging seas, floods. I had only to remember "Praise Him and magnify Him forever". In times of pressure, of uprooting, or worship, this refrain has come alive to me and that has been a joyful thing.

When I have looked down to see the rivers running among the hills and the pools that were filled with water. I recalled Psalms 104 and 107, which came alive.

The waters stood above the mountains. At thy rebuke they fled; at the voice of thy thunder they hasted away. They go up by the mountains; they go down by the valleys until the place which thou hast founded for them. Thou hast set a boundary that they may not pass over; that they turn not again to cover the earth. He sendeth the springs into the valleys, which was among the hills. Psalm 104:6-10

They that go down to the sea in ships, that do business in great waters: These see the works of the Lord, and this wonders in the deep. For he commandeth, and raiseth the stormy wind which lifteth up the waters thereof. They mount up to the heavens, they go down to the depths; their soul is melted because of trouble. They reel to and fro, and stagger like a drunken man, and are at their wits' end. Then they cry unto the Lord in their trouble, and he bringeth them out of their distresses. He maketh the storm a calm, so that the waves thereof are still. Psalm 107:23-29

Flying over the Rockies has given me a very real sense of the hymn, "Oh God, Our Help in Ages Past".

Before the hills in order stood,
Or earth received her frame.
From everlasting Thou art God
To endless years the same.

The Communion Service was very mysterious. There was too much movement, too much to try to follow, too much too soon, too far away. As a child I was fighting in my mind to know what was going on there. In those days he had his back to you. So this is a big improvement for small children. I had too many questions. When the Communion Service was sung, it was a little better, but still it was too long for little children. Matins did not raise so many questions.

Sunday School was the place where we had lessons and where you would normally have asked questions, but it just was not done. We liked the teacher. I do not know if anyone else had so many questions as I did. Take the feeding of the 5,000. I wanted to know where the people came from. I wondered if the whole family had gone out like it was a picnic. But I could not ask questions because I would be embarrassing many, especially the teachers I knew they did not have answers, that I was not going to get the answers I was looking for, so I did not even ask.

I remember the Sunday that the man preached about "God is love." I was a little child, maybe not yet ten years old. I was burning up there when he was saying, "God is love", because every Sunday my brother and I had to go see two old ladies. One was always sick. And you are telling me that God is love and all that? How can God be love and this poor lady is lying down in her bed with this bad pain and is sick all the time.

And then we always had to go and look for a lady by the name of Miss Mary Gill. And she had what I now know to be a varicose ulcer. But all I knew then was that Miss Mary had this sore on her leg. Her features always showed that she was in pain. But we had to go and tell her every Sunday what church was all about

CHAPTER ONE: Growing up in Belize

and so on. And she would send up into the garden to look for whatever fruits were there.

I asked myself what kind of God would have this lady in pain all the time. I had a big argument with myself sitting there when he was telling me that God is love. I could not reconcile a loving God with those two people.

But I could not ask those questions. Who was I going to ask those questions that I had about God's love and suffering? Who could explain that to me? I know that many of my questions they would not answer and they would wonder why I was asking such questions.

I still do not know why Miss Mary had to suffer except that she was heavy and I think she probably did not take care of it until it was far gone. All those kinds of things come clear now, but in those days, you could not tell me that God really loved Miss Mary and she had all that pain—day and night! Why could nobody help her? I was full of questions but could not ask them.

The Good Shepherd

Time moved on and soon I was ready for Shepherd, a kindergarten operated by St. John's Church, with Miss Peachy in Charge. Who could ever forget Miss Peachy? She was pretty and tender, everything a young child would want in a teacher. One memory of those days comes to mind. It is laughable now but it was frightful for me and my friends then.

Miss Peachy told us the story of the Good Shepherd, and then went on to say that God had sent the Bishop to be like the Good Shepherd. All of us were used to seeing the Bishop in church in his robes with his staff and looking to us like our Good Shepherd indeed. He was to visit the school and she wanted us to learn the song. "Loving Shepherd of Thy Sheep," to sing for him. We learned one verse and got ready for the big day.

The big day came! We were to stand up when the Bishop arrived and say, "Good morning, My Lord."

We heard his steps and all stood up, but oh, what a horrible sight. Instead of that wonderful looking person marching up in the beautiful robes with staff in hand, here was an ogre in black clothes with black wrapped around his legs and a funny black hat.

My heart was beating very hard thumping, thumping away and I looked beseechingly at Miss Peachy, who was trying to get us to sing "Loving Shepherd", but all in vain. Somebody started to cry and that did it! Everybody joined in and that was the end of that. How could we explain it to Miss Peachy? Her plans, her looking forward to our big event had turned into a wholly unexpected disaster. We had never seen the Bishop dressed like that, the black hat with its funny shape and his nose looking like it had a great big bend. His voice even sounded like a hiss and nothing Miss Peachy said or did brought us around. I suppose it never dawned on Miss Peachy to tell us what he would be wearing, but I doubt very much that it would have helped.

Big School

Soon it was time to go to the big school. For me, it meant going to my Aunt Annette's private school. Many of my little friends went there, too. One event to do with school stands out. I liked to put on my own underwear and time was when this was a one-piece affair. I put it on buttoned up and went off to school.

Then it happened, I went to do number one, as we said, but I could not undo the buttons and I would not wet my panties. Instead I fainted. The only thing I remember after having made that decision, is waking up when I was almost home to find myself being carried by a man. Dr. Karl Heusner was called and all he did was give two taps and the problem was solved. After that, my mother was very careful to check my underwear and eventually let me wear two-piece underwear instead of the one-piece one.

CHAPTER ONE: Growing up in Belize

The demand for perfection in making our strokes, curves and loops was there. We had a little homework right from the start—a few lines of strokes, then loops, then curves, then putting it together—stroke, the one hook, then a circle that you prettied up, the beginning hook you started with a little tail. It felt like work to get it, but we would get a tick if we had done it right. We all wrote on a framed slate and we had to have a small bottle of water for erasing. To have a tiny perfume bottle was great for the water made things smell good, "sweet", as we used to say.

I often wonder how that use of the word "sweet" came about. Surely, sweet had to do with taste, but in my day and even today, it is still applied to appearance as in "you look sweet", and to smell, as in "you smell sweet". You can even feel sweet. Sweet is a good word.

School had its good points and generally was a good place, except when whippings had to be done. That put me off for a long time. I wanted to cry with everyone who cried, to stand in for anyone who stood there unable to answer. It took me a long time to accept the fact that some people had a learning problem, that some were frightened into forgetfulness. Why didn't everyone learn their lessons so they would not have to be punished?

I tried my best to keep out of the way of scoldings and punishment, but sometimes I forgot to learn my poetry and that meant having to sweep after school, as well as to learn the verse before going home. I stayed away from the whip.

We learned many poems in school—"Little Jim", "We Are Seven", "The Wreck of the Hesperus", "Lucy Gray", "The Inscape Rock", "Casablanca", "Lady Clare", "Elgy in a Country Churchyard". They are all good sound tapes in my mind, put there verse by verse.

The pictures in the readers fascinated me and I used to spend hours looking and seeing and pondering. There were so many little figures, animals, and flowers looking out from those pictures that I do not believe the artists ever realized were there. Even today, pictures open so much extra to my view; carpets and marley coverings keep me fascinated. Tiles also offer good viewing; faces, fish, birds, spring out and there a particular patter, a kind of mosaic that speaks to me of the oneness of humanity. It seems like every nation, every profession, every animal, every shape, is there.

That is how I learned to read tea leaves. I could look in a teacup and see things. There were books that told you what certain symbols meant. If you see a boat that means a person is going to take a trip. My aunt was in charge of the tea booth at the church fairs, but I never told her I could read tea leaves.

The 1931 Hurricane

Patriotism was called forth by the affairs of the Tenth of September. The songs, the marches, the parade to the Barracks and that little paper bag of eats and the pint of lemonade made it worthwhile. Then queen contests and days of festivities were added later. My mother and I made lots of money making cloth hats for the parades because everyone had to have white hats. They looked pretty good when they were starched. Those were the days, or so we thought—until 1931.

I was thirteen when the big hurricane hit on the Tenth of September. There was to be a parade at two o'clock and many school children were there in front of the courthouse ready to march. My Aunt Annette heard about the storm warning and sent her children home. Some did not make it. There was a little boy drowned right there on the corner by our house with his flag still in his hand. But other schools did not even get the message.

There were ninety-some people in our house, up and down. But then we all had to go upstairs. Nurse Vivian Seay from next door was there because their house was gone. It was a good thing she was there

CHAPTER ONE: Growing up in Belize 15

because in the midst of it all there was a baby born. I did not know how it happened, but I just heard the baby cry. Nurse Seay was a great lady. She's the one that started the Black Cross Nurses in Belize.

People in the house were crying because they were separated from their families. I prayed out loud and sang the hymn "Oh God, in a Mysterious Way".

Oh God in a mysterious way
Great wonders you perform
You plant Your footsteps in the sea
And ride upon the storm.

I chanted Psalm 46 over and over, but found no helpers.

"God is our refuge and strength, a very present help in trouble. . . Be still, and know that I am God ... The Lord of Hosts is with us; the God of Jacob is our refuge." Psalm 46: 1, 10, 11

When the tidal wave came it took our house off the posts and settled it on one side. The other windows were intact, but the west ones were gone. I could look through the upstairs west windows and see many houses with no roofs, some on their sides. Our house came through better than most. The house next door also came off its pillars and was moved so close to ours that we could reach out the window and touch it.

Then the wind died down and night came. Aunt Annette was a firm believer in being prepared, so there was kerosene oil and a box of matches under her mattress. We had light and we were dry. It really made me feel good! My Granny had sent us powder bun, johnny cake and Creole bread for the holiday, so we had plenty to eat.

Granny was in Mullins River, not in Belize City, when the hurricane hit. She said she looked out and saw the sea had gone dry. There was only land. The water had been pulled up this way to Belize City in a tidal wave.

We did not know about hurricanes then, about the eye of the storm and it coming around the other side.

St. Johns College before and after the 1931 hurricane in Belize City. Only the staircase in the center remained. (*Courtesy Belize National Archives*)

In the eye of the storm, everyone thought it was over. There was blue sky and no wind. St. John's College was flattened, so many people had come out to help get people out when the tidal wave hit. It was nine feet high and it caught them. That is why so many people drowned in that hurricane.

High School

I went to Dionysian High School, which became St. Hilda's College while I was there and was later renamed Cathedral College. I entered High School in January and then I got malaria right after the May holiday. It came on suddenly and there is no description of those feelings of being thirteen and desperately ill. There

CHAPTER ONE: Growing up in Belize

were bush baths, bitter medicines, and all sorts of treatments for the ague. Food became such a problem since I felt that all I needed to do was to lie there and let what will be, be.

I liked to read, but there was no interest in anything. In odd moments I would ask for something like a ham sandwich, but by the time they sent for it, I did not want it. I went from one bed to another trying to find a place that would do something for my aching body. I did not even want to talk. It was most comforting to have my mother sit on the bed and put my head on her lap. She felt my pain and heartache.

I felt very weak and in my fevered delirium it was as though I would go somewhere where I could not see at all, but could hear children playing far away. I liked that because they played and laughed and sounded so happy.

Then the Principal of my school came to see me, and afterwards she sat in the upstairs parlour talking about my illness. I had been entered for an examination to take place in December, but because of the illness my name was to be taken off the list. I never should have heard that, for it set in me such a sense of hopelessness that I just started crying. I begged them not to take my name off the list as I would be better for the exam. After all, I still had three months. I made such a fuss that they promised to keep my name on the list. But I did not get much better.

By exam time, I felt a little better, but I had to be taken by car as the centre was too far away. A family friend lived nearby and in between times I went there to rest. The day the dictation was to be given, I had the chills so I could not write at all. The examiner was very kind. He came to me and put a chair outside the room so I could sit there. I wanted desperately to take the subject as it was an easy one to pass.

As I was not feeling better, he suggested that I go home, but I told him I would go to my friend's house.

Then, to my amazement and relief, he said he knew I did not want to miss the subject. I was to go to my friend and when the chills went away, I could come over for him to give me the dictation. He made my day and gave me hope. I thanked him and told him I thought I would do all right for the afternoon.

I went to my friend's and told her I would wait a bit so I could take the subject and carry on into the afternoon. I prayed and hoped and after awhile the chills wore off. I managed to finish the exam and went home satisfied that I had done enough to pass.

Back at home I was just as sick as ever and all Christmas I was not the least bit interested in anything. My mother had made me a pretty dress, but I could only look at it and cry. As Easter came, she made me another dress for my birthday, a pretty pink dress, and I asked to put it on, but I could go nowhere. How terrible!

Then I realized that when I went to where the children were, the sounds were louder but I still did not see them. I also began to feel better and started to eat a little. Gradually it came time for me to join the children in their games, but I did not see or hear them any more. It was like part of me was becoming part of them that would see and hear and play and that was all inside of me and I was better.

So I was! By May I was really better and my grandmother promised that if I continued to be well she would let me come for part of the holidays. All of my clothes were too short as I had grown quite a few inches and my mother had to make new clothes and uniforms for me. I was not very strong, but I was able to go for the last three weeks and then back to school in June after the holidays.

It really pleased me that, when the exam results came, I had passed in every subject. The exam was easy and I expected to pass, but the fact that I was able to take it at all gave me great satisfaction.

CHAPTER ONE: Growing up in Belize

I often wondered what the teachers thought who wanted to write me off. But what I learned most of all was extremely important—never to write off anyone. In my teacher years it was really important to me to go all out for those who had been given over to failure. Within the human person there has to be a reachable place, a responsive place, and if we understand that, how many can be saved from the hopeless end to which adults have driven them.

In a lot of ways my high school days were no highlight. I had two very good class friends. One did not finish her final year as she left to get married. I was asked to be godmother to her child but as a high school student, that was unacceptable to both my family and teachers. There were so many "no's" from my family that I got to doing a whole lot of things without telling them. I had to dash from evening classes to the church, which was nearby. The baby was a boy, so I was the only godmother. Girls have two godmothers.

I had given no thought to who the godfathers would be and there, with baby in hand, I proceeded to join the two godfathers, only to discover that my uncle was one! I was already nervous for this was my first godchild and then I also had to deal with the opposition to my being a godmother! I was not in very good shape to hold the child. I was really shaking, but once I realized it was all right with my uncle and the priest, I felt better and got through the ceremony. Of course, news got home and I was severely reprimanded by my aunts, but the deed had already been done. My mother understood, but as usual, she had nothing to say.

Many of the unpleasant things in my life were from family rivalries. My youngest aunt, Aunt Nora, was very jealous of me. She was smart, the first to learn Touch Typing. She worked for the church, but it was not a profession. Although later she did go on to nursing.

After I graduated, I wanted to teach, but my Aunt Annette wanted me to wait awhile before I started working. I knew of a vacancy at the Cathedral School and applied anyway. What I did not know was that the letter would be considered by the church committee on which my aunt sat! She said she did not know that I had applied, so I got no job. That was that! But how does a young adult handle such a thing? The Chairperson of the committee was really upset by the whole affair for he was sure I would get the job. He sent for me the next day and tried to explain, but the only explanation I wanted was that he would recommend me for another job. Whatever the job, I needed to work. My mother was unhappy about it, too, but she was not the boss, and she had to go along with it.

The next day, I went to see if I could get a Christmas job at Brodie's, a department store that handles many types of merchandise. All I needed was a recommendation, which the priest gave me. I got the job, but said nothing to anyone, not even to my mother and grandmother, as much as I loved them.

The following Monday, I got up as usual, had my breakfast and on my way out, I made the announcement that I was going to work at Brodie's. I waited for no reaction and set out for a job I knew I would not like, but which I needed to establish my independence.

When I came home at lunchtime, the silence was dreadful. I did not want any food, so I went into the room where my mother would be. She fully understood and she felt for me.

I stayed with the job and on payday I bought something for everyone, including a hat for my grandmother. She was pleased, as was my mother to whom I gave $2.

By and by things eased up and eventually they condescended to give me a list of things we needed for Christmas. I could buy cheaply there. I did not apply to continue working in the New Year as I was sure I could get a teaching job. My aunt had a big school and I could have been of much help to her, but I gave up on the idea of working there. I dreamed and hoped that I could get a good job so that my mother, brother, and I could rent somewhere for ourselves, but my mother was not in favour of such an idea. Little did I dream the New Year would bring me the cruellest experience of all, the loss of my mother.

My Brother Frederick

From the beginning I was my Aunt Annette's baby. I slept in her bed. But my brother was treated quite differently. My mother had to take care of him. He slept downstairs with her. He never felt accepted by my aunts.

My aunt paid for my education and could have afforded to send him to school, but she did not. My brother was really smart, but he never got over the fact that I went to high school and he did not. He was sent to St. Mary's night school because it was all my mother could afford. Then he went to Jack Flowers who trained him well as a cabinetmaker. His work was outstanding, but he never accepted his ability.

My brother's handwriting was full of points and jagged edges and showed his deep psychological condition. Once in Chicago I went to a lecture on children's handwriting and learned there just how much parents and teachers can learn about the inner nature of their little ones. All sorts of little clues were there, some relating to physical conditions. Nervous children could not be missed for when blown up, their writing showed a series of dots Some writing had both dots and short lines. The group doing the research hoped to keep up their study of a number of children whose handwriting showed that they might have physical, mental, psychological or social problems. The group was not recommending that every child's writing be analysed but where some things are very different or obvious, a study could be helpful while the child is still young. Points and jagged edges like my brother's writing were clear. Even as a youngster he was always in trouble, very irritable and never satisfied with home.

He became an alcoholic and I well remember how it all started. There was to be a birthday party somewhere and a family friend, much older than my brother, came to ask for him to go. He went and I cannot forget how they had to bring him home, lifting him up and putting him in bed. My mother was shocked as was I. He was sixteen at the time. It is so sinful and unkind for older ones to lead the young astray.

Had my brother accepted his own gifts, he could have had a very good life, but it seemed that he was bent on destroying mine. I went through terrible days with him and nights were worse than days. I longed to see him delivered so he could find happiness. Although we lived in the same house, he would never accept food from me.

When I went to Seminary for a Master's degree, it was more than he could stand, so he sold every single thing in my house. That was painful to me, but more so the fact that it was bought by some of my neighbours!

I am very grateful to Beverly Felix, who really cared about my brother. He cared about her, too, and would listen to her when I could not go near. He had two severe nervous breakdowns and he accepted caring from everyone but me. I was really the enemy.

Beverly first came around to help me with household chores and errands. She was eight years old and really wanted to stay with me all the time. I did not feel led to do that, so she stayed until after supper, did her homework and went home to sleep. Beverly was such a caring child and she was very fond of my brother. Often when he was drunk, she would fix his food since he ate well, drunk or sober.

Beverly was a wonderful person to have around and she helped me through many difficulties with my brother. She went through grade school and then to the Technical College and did very well. Later on she got a job in one of the big stores, but she still helped me.

CHAPTER ONE: Growing up in Belize

The great break for her came when I took an exchange group of ten persons to British Columbia. She was one of four teenagers in the group. On the way back, she stopped off in Los Angeles to spend time with a sister who was a nurse there. That was it. She stayed there, got married, later divorced, got into the navy, married again to someone in the Navy and they had two children.

People called my brother Mr. Eric, but his name was Frederick, and the family and his friends called him Rico. When my brother had money everyone else would get it, but if he ever gave me money, he would be back for it, so I just put up any money he offered me. Wishful thinking does not change things, but I wish that our relationship could have been better.

He was an alcoholic and thought he had a bad heart, but the last week of his life, the doctor told him he had emphysema. When he told me of it, he said, "I have the same thing Breshnev had and there is no cure for that."

The doctor asked him about his work and learned that he had been a cabinet-maker. Fine sawdust started the problem with his lungs and smoking added to it.

My brother never had one good word to say about our father. Shortly before he died he said,

"I want to tell you something. I have been very bad to you and I always wanted to make it up to you, but I know now I won't. I know you forgave me long ago, but I have told God all about everything, even the old man (our father) and asked him to forgive all my sins. I feel all right now."

When my brother was to pass away, I was lying in bed one morning and dozed off. I saw a coffin in the front room and went to see who was in it—my brother. The dream continued and I saw another coffin. Again I went to look and it was my Aunt Kathleen this time. He died eleven days after I had the dream and she died 20 days later. I knew he was ill, but still his death came quite quickly, only three weeks after our conversation about his talking to God and asking for forgiveness.

My Father

I hardly knew my father because he went away when I was very young. It was only as an adult when he returned that I came to know him. He told me about his alcoholism. He used to drink hard, as he put it, but one day he was all alone and overwhelmed by his whole lifestyle. He wept for my mother, for us, for his other family (three children older than we were), for his mother, and for the rest of the family. He knelt down in the open and prayed for forgiveness and asked God to deliver him from alcohol.

He rose up, never took another drink, and gave God the praise and glory. He told me that he always prayed for me in special ways because he knew, even before I was born, that I was a special child. The night I was born the midwife was sitting on the porch talking with my aunt. She told them, "This is a very special child that is being born tonight."

He deeply regretted not being part of my growing up years, but as Tennyson wrote,

"I know there are no errors
In the great eternal plan;
And all things work together
For the final good of man."

My father and I became closer after he lost his sight. He told me about the lumber industry and that lumber cut during the new moon should not be used. The sap was always lowest then, and this wood would rot quickly in the tropical climate and had to be replaced every three years. Wood cut at other times lasted much longer.

He was very interested in science and environmental issues, although we did not call them that back then. He also liked land. He had some land on the Sibun River but after he lost his sight, he gave that up.

My mother's marriage was a great disappointment and long after she died, my father told me he regretted not being able to tell her he was sorry for his treatment of her. He never explained anything to me nor did I ask him, but one thing of great value to me was that I was a wanted child. Whatever he did, I forgave him, but my brother never set him free until three weeks before he died.

A Living Stream

My mother and I used to have little chats and I felt good when we did. She liked me to play hymns on Sunday afternoons and one of her favourites was "A Living Stream".

A living stream as crystal clear
Welling from the throne of God
And of the Lamb of God
The Lord to man hath shown
Faith sees and hears but oh for wings
That we might taste and feel
Lord of the ark, put forth thy hand
And take the wanderers in.

My mother had an awareness where her children were concerned. In my early life my brother and I liked to play pillow fight. One day we were upstairs horsing it out when he got that pillow over my head. He was shouting that he had won and I was going somewhere sweet and easy.

Later my mother told me she suddenly realized we were very quiet and she rushed upstairs to find him with the pillow over my face and me lying there very still. She grabbed me up and ran over to Nurse Seay next door who worked on me and managed to bring me back to consciousness. For me it was just like waking up from a long sleep. We never played pillow fight again. My mother spoke of an awareness that told her the quiet was not good, that there was danger and she did what she had to do.

"A little more and you would have been gone" was how she put it.

My mother was a very special kind of person. Everyone at home knew it. Outside people knew it and I believe I knew it more than anyone else. She was good, kind, honest truthful, thoughtful, caring, and soft, a lover of peace. This was how everybody experienced her and she was the servant of all. She was beloved by aunts and uncles who called her "Daughter", and by all the in-laws.

Many people came to her with their troubles for she was a good listener. Visitors came in the evening, and now and then she took us out in the late evening to visit certain people. She was very fond of my father's only sister and we really liked going there.

I wondered about my mother's feelings. Was her life to be just work and work and work? She did not have to wash, but she cooked and sewed and was very quiet. She kept all the letters my father wrote, but she never answered them, at least not to my knowledge.

She was a dressmaker with a chain stitch machine, but sometimes my dresses did not get done. The morning of a day I was to go to a birthday party, my dress had not even been touched. I cut it out with her help and she sewed it so that by five o'clock I was ready. We made it plain and put one panel in the front for style.

One Saturday when I was eighteen, we were sitting on the back steps talking and she said, "I am going away."

I laughed because going away meant Mullins River where my grandmother was, and the only way to get there was by boat. That meant a happy outing. My mother could not stand too many ripples at the foreshore and she stayed away from boats. I told her that wherever she went I would be going, for a fish could not swim without its tail.

"You'll see," was the response.

We got up and went inside. Next evening, she said she wanted me to go with her to the doctor as she felt feverish. We went and she was given some medicine. She did not look sick, but she did have a fever that the doctor diagnosed as malaria. Two days after she took the medicine, her skin broke into shilling-sized blotches. In a few days her long beautiful hair started falling out. It suddenly dawned on me that my mother was talking about leaving me, about dying. She was quiet as usual and took very little food. She was slowly leaving us and she knew it. We did not believe it.

The night before she died, she sent me to call the Church Army Evangelist and she had a long talk with him. Then she called me in and said she told him everything and he would tell me, but she did want me to stay at home and work. She had done enough for my brother and me, and I understood what she meant. She had to do what she did because of us, my brother and me, and had paid the price for whatever had been done for us. I promised her I would listen and heed her words.

She told her sisters she was ready to go and they wanted to know if she was forgetting us. She was not. She had taken care of all that. They wanted to call in the priest and she said there was no need as the time for that was over.

Early the next morning she called for my brother and me. He was on her left and she put out her hand to him. I was on her right and she put out her right hand to me. "I am going now," she said, "Be good and trust God to care for you."

It was all over. All over! Death is so cruel at times and no one is truly prepared for it. The grief that overcame me was unbelievable. Everyone was crying uncontrollably because the tie was broken; she had really held the family together.

She had always wanted to be buried the same day if possible. Since her passing was so early in the day, it could be done, so it was. She had a good funeral and her special hymn was sung.

My father had been told that she was sick and he tried to get home before she died, but she was already gone before he arrived. I did not see him then for I was not at home. I was so overwhelmed by grief that I was put in the hands of a very precious friend, Mrs. Ella Craig. She was my special adult friend and had been a good advisor in my times of distress. I could not keep myself together at all. I wanted to run, to scream, to tear myself apart. I was aware that I had lost control of myself.

I was a long, long time returning to my natural state of peace and quiet and the great trauma was that I did not really love those around me. I felt that they were the ones who had prevented the true mother-daughter relationship. My mother had yielded her rights to us for our own sakes because of her dependence. It must have been extremely painful for her to be a mother, yet to do very little mothering. Still I had to recognize what had been done for me. I could hold a job and earn a living because I had been cared for.

I became deeply attached to some missionaries and knew that some time they would go away. I had to get ready to go, too, and I did, very much against the wishes of my family.

But it did not work out the way I wanted. In the wisdom of Almighty God, I was not supposed to return home. He saw to it that once I got to Jamaica there was neither ship nor plane to take me home and Jamaica became home for me. With my mother gone, I was glad not to return. It would be ten years before I would return, even for a visit.

Chapter Two
Jamaica
(1941-43)

But when we got to Jamaica, there was no way to get to British Honduras because of the war. Here I was, wanting to go home yet knowing that this was presently impossible, for Jamaica had no travel links with British Honduras in those war days. I had to adapt to these circumstances, live through them without being swallowed by them.

In Transit in Barbados

In Belize the Anglican Church had an evangelical group called the Church Army, which had the Better Brigade, a youth training program. They went on missions, visiting prisons, mental hospitals, the infirmary, and the sick. The Church Army training had a test with lots of scriptures. They were happy with my visiting, but not with my knowledge of the scriptures. They said I was not ready. Much later Bishop Smith told me,

"The Church Army wasn't for you, too many rules and regulations."

But at the time I wanted to go on a foreign mission with the Church Army. Two years after my mother died, my aunt decided to let me go. So, when I was twenty-one years old, I left British Honduras with this Anglican mission group headed for Trinidad.

On the outward journey, bound for Trinidad, we spent a couple of days in Jamaica. I was hosted by the Soutar family. Members of this family held high positions in the government and they had a house with seventeen rooms.

From there we went on to Barbados, but insurmountable problems arose which caused me to remain in Barbados for three months. Bishop Bentley was very caring of me. He was not satisfied with the home where I was staying and saw to it that I was able to stay with three nuns in the Anglican Convent at St. Michael's. They were also kind and tender with me and I began to feel quite alive there. They had very good food and I fitted easily into the life there, even the meals eaten in silence.

St. Michael's Cathedral had a Boys' Choir that was out of this world. Nearly everyone had their own vegetable garden. I spent a lot of time with the family next door to the Convent. They were in education and had Masters' degrees. Barbados was very uplifting because the families were so into education. It offered some things about life I had never met before, such as a relatively high standard of living for all social classes.

I found my way to what was known as the Girls' Industrial Union, where you paid very little to learn something and just stayed until you learned it. It was a skills training centre and I was ready for something like that. You could learn almost any kind of needlework or knitting there. I learned tatting, which they taught with coarse thread so you could learn much quicker. I also learned hardanger, a Scandinavian kind of needlework. I even learned to make lemon drops. It was very crowded because people stopped after work, a wonderful place.

St. Michael's was a big parish and there was much to do. I went with the nuns on their missions and learned a lot. Each day, the nuns would go over the scriptures we would use when we went to visit the sick.

CHAPTER TWO: Jamaica

They went out every day alone, I got to see quite a bit. Before I left, they asked me if I did not want to stay.

However, the greatest thing happened to me one Sunday when the Sisters were slated to go to a small church to show lantern slides on the Passion. On Saturday everyone went to bed apparently feeling quite well. The next morning two were sick and by noon no one was around. They rested from two until four pm and at four o'clock, when no one got up, I went to see about them. They were all sick and unable to go anywhere. At five o'clock Mother Nun rang her bell and I went to see what she wanted.

"Child," she said, "you know we are to be at the mission this evening. As you see, we are all sick. None of us can go. My child, you are the only one who is well. You will have to go because the people will be waiting." She picked up her phone and called for the person who was to take them. He was to come right away as it was late already. I was very reluctant because I did not think I could do it alone. "You know the story," she said reassuringly, "Just tell the story with the slides." I was nervous about going, but I got ready and went to tell her I was leaving. "Yes," she said, "it is late. I know the people are waiting."

They were indeed waiting. The little church was full. She had given me a program that started with a hymn. I was to introduce myself and explain why the Sisters could not be there, then do the slideshow. Everything was fine except for one slide, "The Father on his sapphire throne."

I have never visualized God as a person, a grey-haired man on a throne. But I showed the picture and we closed the event with another hymn. I guess I did all right because after that someone thanked me on behalf of everyone and asked me to come again. I had done nothing like this before, but God helped me do it. I was in the right place at the right time. I know also that those three nuns really held me in prayer and I learned something about readiness and about doing what one could do.

As a Quaker, Stephen Grellet once said, "I shall pass through this world but once. Any good thing I can do, let me not defer it nor neglect it for I shall not pass this way again."

Now and then circumstances arise that take me back to that Sunday. I still see Mother Nun as she checked the time and I hear the urgency in her voice.

"It is late. I know the people are waiting." I think of how someone is always waiting. The word of God knows its best moment, but it waits for a willing heart. We are the means by which it is done.

Kingston—Looking for Work

I went to Trinidad, but I only stayed one week. I cannot say what turned me off. It was something I sensed, some kind of undercurrent. I was going back home by way of Jamaica, first to Baranquilla, Colombia, by sea plane and then to Jamaica by ship. But when we got to Jamaica, there was no way to get to British Honduras because of the war. Here I was, wanting to go home yet knowing that this was presently impossible, for Jamaica had no travel links with British Honduras in those war days.

I had to adapt to these circumstances, live through them without being swallowed by them. As soon as I realized the Jamaican mindset, I just got into that mindset. You had to push your way there. I came to love Jamaica.

Fortunately, I could stay with my great-aunt who was living in Kingston—my mother's aunt, Matilda Brown Sealey. She had lived many years in Cuba. She had one son, Theodore Sealey, who had the best education. He was editor of the newspaper, the *Daily Gleaner*. She had a beautiful yard full of fruit trees in the back, and ferns and flowers in the front. She also had an area fenced off for her poultry. She generated quite

CHAPTER TWO: Jamaica 33

a bit of cash as people bought flowers, ferns, chochos, peppers, okras and fruits from her. Her son took good care of her, but it was good that she could be busy with her own projects. The house was large enough so she rented part of it, but found renters to be troublesome as she was a very particular person. My aunt did all her own work, so I learned to work Jamaican style. In a short time I could fix up a floor shining bright, staining it with red ochre and shining it with a coconut brush. It was hard work, but the floor really did look good.

I found it difficult to feel at home though she really tried her best. The only other people I knew were her son and the family that I had met on the way to Trinidad, but they were far away.

The alternative was to find a job. I tried working as a dressmaker's helper but that was no good. The neighbour suggested that I try Luke Lane. That meant working in a store and trying to exist in a very noisy environment. I lasted two weeks. The lady in charge told me I should try it for a longer time as I would get used to it. Who wants to get used to that?

My system was just not built to absorb the noises of those competing for the all-important pounds, shillings, and pence, to keep the economy going. Western Kingston, Luke Lane, Princess Street, Spanish Town Road, and Coronation Market were the noisiest places in the whole of Jamaica, yet they had a fascination of their own.

I wondered if those who worked there would give it up if other jobs were available. But I learned that among the buying and selling and all the haggling that went on, many preferred the street selling because it gave them independence. They were accountable only to themselves.

This type of marketing was new to me. As I bought something and opened doors to a one-to-one experience with sellers, I found out about people's sense of themselves, their hopes and fears, their troubles, and their religious ideas. Often they became givers, they wanted to give me a bit more than I had bought. Most people had troubles and most had little schooling. Many were concerned about their children and wanted them to go to school. They did not go to church because they did not have the right clothes, but they believed in the Lord.

Sometimes they sold out and at other times they made very little, but they each claimed a special spot. People on corners sold more than others did. Many women could crochet and had a damp rag to wipe off their fingers. Some carried their noon meal. If they had to leave their spot, they covered their boxes or asked other sellers to take care of things.

After I gave up the job I prayed for help because I needed to get away from the situation in which I found myself. My great-aunt really believed that something was not right with me and she decided to take certain steps that put an end to our troubled relationship. She was right in a way I did not understand at the time.

One morning she told me she wanted me to go with her to see a friend. When we got there, she told the woman she wanted her to help me. I was given a seat at a small table and a lighted candle was put near a Bible. The lady stood behind me, told me to close my eyes and then she put her hands on my head.

After a while she started to speak what she was seeing. She spoke of my father and how he had fallen into a pit that an enemy had dug for him. I was in grave danger for this was to affect me and I needed protection and deliverance. She told me to write out a Psalm and keep it on me all the time for the next nine days and I should return on the tenth day.

We returned home and I was told how much the venture cost and I should pay up. I was angry over the whole thing and refused to pay. This was a terrible thing to do and, though I realized that she meant well, I decided against paying.

CHAPTER TWO: Jamaica

Things went from bad to worse. As I was locked out, I slept on one of the benches in the front yard. At 2 a.m. she opened the door and called me in. I went in because I was cold, but I slept with my head on the table.

The old lady was hurt and she wept bitterly for she said she was only trying to help me and I did not realize how serious my situation was. A bad spirit had troubled her and she had fainted in church. I did not buy the bad spirit story because she had gone to church without even a cup of tea.

I fixed a cup of hot tea, which she drank, and we both spent the morning crying. We did not eat for the whole day and I only took a glass of lemonade before going to bed, I knew I had to find a job and move away from this place.

I tried to get out of it by going with the Adventists. They had a campaign going in Kingston at that time. At first they so enthralled me that I nearly became an Adventist. Then I had a dream.

I could hear singing. I tried to go toward the Adventists where the singing was coming from, but there were thorns and thistles. I had a hard time getting through. An angel put a hand on my shoulder and said to go back the way I came. The bush opened up for me to go back.

I took the dream as a sign that I should leave the Adventists alone.

I looked in the newspaper and saw an ad for a teacher. I had no papers with me but thought I would try anyway. I told my great-aunt what I wanted to do, but she said I would never get the job because Jamaica was a place that wanted qualified people and I had no papers.

I sent an application and waited. Then one day the postman brought me a letter that I opened quickly. It said that on a certain date the Principal of the Infant School at Carron Hall, Ms. T, would come and see me.

She came and we looked at the snags. She needed a teacher very badly and wanted me to have the job. She told me she would speak to an education officer and gave me the name of Ruby Meredith. I was to go to the Education Office for an interview with her. Once I was successful, I would fill out a form and she would do the rest. Then, if all went well, I would get a letter from the Manager of the Infant School at Carron Hall.

Fortunately, Eric Brown, a Jamaican who was the Education Officer of British Honduras was in Jamaica at the time. So, he wrote a recommendation for me.

Ms. T encouraged me to take the job. It was a probationer's job, which paid four pounds monthly. She usually charged five pounds for room and board, but in view of my situation, she would charge me only three pounds. It sounded terrible, but it was better than Luke Lane and I would be away from a bad home situation.

My great-aunt was surprised that I was even considered and she never said much to me because of the money she thought I owed her. I did not have that kind of money anyway, for I had spent the Luke Lane money on a pair of shoes.

The next week was bad and my great-aunt threatened to go to my friend, Ernestine, on East Street. I had met Ernestine on my way to Trinidad. She was the Soutar's aunt and lived in the back of their house. She had been a successful social worker but had fallen on hard times. I had many good conversations with her. When I did not have bus fare, I walked the distance to her house and she always gave me the fare home. She had very little for herself though she had known better times.

When my great-aunt came home from her Saturday marketing, she told me she was feeling sick. She had planned to stop in to tell Ernestine how I would not pay what she thought I owed her, but when she tried to put her hand on the gate, she could not do it. She felt a spirit prevented her. I felt sorry for her.

CHAPTER TWO: Jamaica

I had gone to the Education Office and found Ruby Meredith extremely helpful to me. I had a good conversation with her and I promised not to let her down. I knew then that the Manager would accept me, so I waited for his letter that came a week after my interview. He wrote me an encouraging letter and gave me a starting date. I showed my aunt the letter and she said I was lucky.

I had a few possessions but prepared to take my leave of the old lady. She gave me money for bus fare and ten shillings. I had no other money. So it was that a whole new phase of existence began when I took the bus for Carron Hall via Highgate.

Next to the Wall

The bus was very crowded and, as this was my maiden voyage into Jamaica's country life, it was somewhat exciting. There were market people going home with lots of baskets—bankra baskets, they were called. People pushed and pulled, cursed and swore, and threatened, like this was how it had to be to get your rights.

If you looked too hard at someone, maybe just out of interest, it was, "Look ya, lady, ne mek me an you have nutting. Tek you eye offa me."

"Good heavens," I thought, "how could people be this way?" And yet, beneath all of it, one could feel the heartbeat of Jamaica. There was quite a bit of humour and such subtleties.

Someone came by the window with a candy bar and I could not resist coconut cake—pink and white and ginger sweet. Taking very small bites, and allowing myself to savour it well, two of each would go a long way. I was really hungry but I dared not take more than two shillings out of the ten.

The bus took very long to move off, but when I heard a great blast on the horn and the conductor came in and took his place, I knew that the journey into the unknown had begun.

What a ride it was! The sights to be seen on the roadside and what went on inside the bus kept my eyes and ears rather busy. Spanish Town was the first big stop.

"Hallelujah, my Lord, what is this?" I thought.

After more pushing and pulling, we were off again. Every now and then I laughed it off. I had a book as I supposed anyone who wondered what I was laughing at would conclude that I was laughing at something I had read.

Then I heard about the Junction Road. What a road to travel by bus! These gullies were very threatening to my faith and when one bus had to pass another, it was to ask yourself, how? However, before I knew it, the manoeuvre was completed and with honking horns we flew along.

Then on this, my first bus ride, the bus broke down. We were to arrive at Highgate at three o'clock, so I could catch the four o'clock bus to Carron Hall. No such luck. The bus coughed and choked and issued terrible odours that nauseated me. I was in the second row and if it was bad there, think what it was for those in the back! Passengers were really unhappy. It was Saturday and everybody wanted to get home.

To crown it off, we did not get to Highgate until 11 o'clock and the driver said the bus was done for. "Well now, what next," I thought. I watched the Jamaicans get off and disappear. Everyone went somewhere and I was the only one still sitting on the bus.

"Lady, you have to get off the bus." I stayed put.

He went across the street to the bar, the only thing still open. He came back and rapped on the window and repeated, "Lady, you have to get off the bus."

I had to talk to God for this man really meant it. I said silently, "Lord, you heard the man say I have to get off the bus. If I have to, then you must know where I am to go."

CHAPTER TWO: Jamaica

The driver walked back to the bar and complained loudly to the barman, who came over to the bus, "Lady, it look like you got troubles. You no noh nobody round ya?"

"No, I am going to Carron Hall to teach and I can't get the bus until tomorrow." My speech bought me some sympathy.

"Driver, dis lady da no Jamaican, mek we see wah we can do fa help her. Hold on, Lady," he said, and proceeded up the road.

In a short time he was back with a lady. "I told my wife about your troubles, and how you is a stranger. Our house is very small, but you are welcome to it."

So he took my suitcase and came back for the box with books and a few prized possessions. I had a small overnight bag which she took from me.

"This is all you tings?"

"Yes," I said, and she said, "Come then, let's go. We just live three houses up the road."

He finally introduced himself, "My name is Dan and my wife is Lilla, but I call her Val."

So, I went along and small was really small. Still it was a shelter. He went to close up the bar and she went to fix up something for me to eat.

"You must be hungry," she said. I was. "I have to fix something for Dan, too, so make yourself at home."

I saw no solution to the sleeping problem. The little house was spick and span. She was such a neat person. He was, too, and I sensed something good going on between them.

In a little while she told me to come for what she had prepared. Bread and butter, some kind of jam, and something hot to drink that did not look or smell like anything I had ever seen, but I would have to drink it. The taste was really terrible, but I swallowed it quickly and depended on the bread and jam to kill the taste. It was soroci tea with milk and she offered me some more. I refused gracefully.

While I was having the food, she was busy inside and I began to wonder if there was a part of the house I could not see. Her husband came in and she served his share.

"Come," she said, "let me show you where you will sleep." She led the way to the bedroom. "Put your clothes over the foot of the bed," and she showed me the washing up situation. The water and basin were on one of those ledges served by a push out board window and the bucket was handy.

But that fourposter bed was a sight! She had changed the sheets and pillowcases. Everything was starched and lily white!

She said, "you will sleep next to the wall. I will sleep next to you and Dan will sleep next to me." Homesickness burst upon me like a top-gallon flood, so I went to the front door that was still open to get hold of myself. I was grateful as much as I could be, but the "next to the wall" affair was quite another matter. I dried my tears, said good-night, thanks, and went into the room, knelt down to say my prayers only to be homesick—bad, bad, bad! I had my nightie on and stood by the little push-out window. I washed my face again and felt better. I climbed into bed, turned my face to the wall and truly, the Lord gave me a deep sleep. I never heard them get into the bed, nor did I wake when they got out of bed in the morning. What if I had had to use the bucket in the night? The Lord was so good it was not required.

When I woke it was broad daylight. She was outside singing "And Can It Be." When she came to the end of it, I called out to tell her how beautiful her voice was and that she should sing more. She sang "Master Speak, Thy Servant Heareth" and I knew she had to be a Methodist. I was not ready to get up, so she sang

CHAPTER TWO: Jamaica

one more—a hymn called "My God I am Thine." I had not heard that before, but when she got to "My heart it doth dance at the sound of Thy name," I felt the joy of it. The tune and the words went together so well. I had to get up for I felt light and good and well rested. She came into the house and offered me breakfast—roasted breadfruit, which I was having for the first time, and a bit of codfish in coconut oil. She poured out the tea—soroci tea with milk again. I hurried it down and set to this codfish and breadfruit. I was well fixed for the morning. She told me how to roast a breadfruit, one of my very important learnings. To this day I enjoy roasted breadfruit, the only difference being that I use a gas fire and not wood.

"Go see the town," she said. "No bus will pass till four o'clock."

I did and saw the beauty of hills and valleys, rivers and streams, of people, some obviously well-to-do and others trying to do well without. There were beautiful gardens everywhere. These people really loved beauty. I sat on a huge boulder and felt the unity with all things creep into all of me.

A little old lady came and sat on the stone with me. She was resting while waiting on the boy to come along with the donkey. Soon he rounded the curve and they went on towards the market.

When I got back Val was cooking. She baked her bread and was fixing a box for me to take. I told her I was on my way to Carron Hall.

"What school?" She asked

"Carron Hall Infant School," I said.

"They don't keep no teacher there," she said, "Every minute they leave, she's just miserable." She asked how many sheets I had. "Two sheets, two pillow cases," I said, so she put more linens in my box.

"Guess what," she said, "somebody is here from Carron Hall and Dan asked for a ride for you, so they'll pick you up after five o'clock. Look, you can't go to Ma T. empty-handed. I have fixed up some things for you to take—oranges, coconuts, grapefruit, carrots and gungo peas. I'll put some more in for Ms. T. That will make her feel good."

"Let her know you have somebody here. Don't let her take advantage of you, for you are too easy to work with her."

I thought to myself, that it would possibly be very difficult for Ms. T. to deal with me for I could keep her outside of me and not get into internal tangles. Maybe she had never had that kind of challenge. I needed her as much as she needed me, so I knew we were going to make it in spite of the way people saw her. I was not buying what was said. Had I not met her? I could sense some tension but she accepted me and helped me get into the system.

Val and I had a good lunch. I had a nap and went into the town with my friend who really took me into her heart. She had always wanted a sister and now God had sent her one. She was happy with me. She introduced me to all the shopkeepers and the store people. The market folk had gone and the town was quiet. Some teachers were in town and she introduced me to them. We went into the bar to hail Dan who said he'd be over when I was ready to go.

We went back to the little house and she set about baking some bread that she had left to rise while we were out. She had an outside kitchen for such things so I stayed just by the door where I would not get smoky. She told me about her parents who lived about ten miles away, so they saw each other often. She had not gone to High School in Port Maria as it was far away; and anyway, they did not have the money. She had a term at Conti—short for Continuation School, but her father got ill and she had to leave, so she got married when she was seventeen. Now she was thirty-

CHAPTER TWO: Jamaica

five and Dan was forty. They had been very happy, but they had no children. Dan was from a large family who also cared about her. She did not shop for fruits and vegetables and many times she got meat of some kind from them. There was such a wholesomeness about these two people.

At four o'clock Dan came over to check if everything was all right and soon a car drove up. He introduced me to the bank officer for agricultural loans, Mr. Boyd, who would take me right to Ms. T's place. I saw that he looked like the Boyds in Belize. He was their uncle.

At parting time I felt that years had passed since Val and I met, and I hoped for a long friendship with her. I had already forgotten about Kingston. Except for one dear lady, Ernestine, I had not made any real fiends and had set down no roots. Everything from this point was in one direction, here to there, and this short break in the journey was very good. Next stop, Carron Hall.

Carron Hall

Life at Carron Hall was unlike anything I had ever experienced before. I had to share a small room with another teacher. There was only a narrow space between the two single beds, one chest of drawers for both, and very little space for hanging clothes.

There was a door leading to the dining room and one leading outside to the back of the house, so I could get into the yard easily. The house was right by the street side so all the traffic noises were heard. The main road led to Carron Hall proper and another branched off to the villages that lay beyond the Presbyterian church and schools—Infant, Primary and the Home Economics Training Centre, a place widely known for quality training.

The road also led, in the other direction, to Highgate, the place where I slept next to the wall. Carron Hall was beautifully situated but it was very damp.

Ms. T was really glad to see me and she was very pleased with my offerings. She introduced me to the other teacher, Ms. James. She showed me around and went out saying she would soon be back. Ms. James seemed to be waiting for a listening ear. She described how Ms. T was worried when I did not come as expected, but she heard about the bus breaking down and hopes revived.

Ms. James said, "This place is a real hole and it's like living at the end of it—a dead end hole I mean." She was going to leave at the end of the term. I asked her if Ms. T knew and she said she had told her when she came that she would only stay one year.

"We quarrel every day—the food is terrible—this everlasting mutton soup, sardines, cheese, and as for tea"—she kissed her teeth—two Marie biscuits and one cup of tea every day. Breakfast makes me mad— half raw cornmeal, a small piece of cheese or a piece of codfish smaller than your little finger, or else one sardine! Scrambled eggs all the time, like one egg for two of us. Maybe you will get better treatment."

Now she broke into patois. "No nevah see nuttin like dis before. Watch it tomorrow. Big Sunday, you watch what we gwine get. How much you gwine pay?"

"I am not sure yet because I have to work under grade P" I explained.

"Lord," she exclaimed, "P pay and live here! You noh gwine have nuttin fo yourself, if me and you gwine pay de same ting. In fact, dat no gwine work because I pay my hand five fo dis! But you da stranger and you no gwine get it fo pay her, so ah no gwine say nuttin. We really wan wa nex teacher. Good ting you come. You and she gwine get on. Me glad de las one never stay because it was war every day. Look ya me can' fine one good ting fo tell you bout Ms. T but every puss get e own luck. You jus come but me done see dat you too sof' for work ya. You noh look like you even know how fo quarrel."

CHAPTER TWO: Jamaica

I had never thought that was something one knew how to do.

"All I can tell you is dis—no mek she tek no advantage a you. Anyway, me wa de right ya."

I remembered Val's words.

"Go rest yourself. I do wait pon de bus, as me clothes come up every week and de bus carry it same time. Ah sen one box and ah get one and I get few things fo eat, but I keep it right in da box pon da shelf eena da room."

I went to the room, opened the door into the yard and saw a woman and a girl sitting on the step. The woman was May, the cook and washer and she, too, was waiting for a listening ear.

You is Ms. Vernon, neh. Ms T tell me about you from the day she see you in Kingston. Nearly every day she called your name, hoping you noh change you mind."

"Cass, this lady is the new teacher." And to me she said, "she da mi one lee gal but a head only hard—maybe you can help me wid her. Ms James mi try, but she give up. We da maroon, no se we colour and we frizzy hair—like e wan straight, but yet a frizzy like?" She laughed.

"Go fine sometin to do eena da room," she told the girl. Then she remembered she needed something from the shop. "You want anything, teacher?" I did not and she sent the child off. I already knew that she was going to educate me about things.

"Ms James must be done tell you everything." She stated. I gave no response, so she went on.

"She da trouble too so mind yourself wid her. I no say Ms. T no mean and got bad ways. No see how she talk, e top lip no move at all and e talk through e teeth and e lips dem thin, thin. E can' help it, e born wid bad temper. Everybody and she quarrel. I do work ya long time but I really would want another work. Too much find fault go on and ah get nuff. De only reason why I stay wid her is that me and mi lee gal can live here. We get lee bit a feed an we de close to de school. If Ms. T like you, you noh got nuttin fo worry bout. If she no like you is like macca de eena you clothes."

"Dat las teacher beat anything I ever see. Sometimes is like de wan fight. She shoulda nevah come ya. Ms. T say she no gwine tek one next teacher widout'n she see dem and talk wid dem. No see, she gone way da you house da Kingston fo see you before she till Reverend to hire you."

"I believe you wan' stan' good wid her. From da time she come fun town she da talk bout you and she boasting bout dis teacher we come from some way—me really glad you come."

It was a quiet Sunday. Ms. James invited me to go with her to spend the day with some friends at a nearby village, but Ms. T had already invited me to go to church and I promised to go.

"We leave here ten o'clock. Church is at eleven."

Breakfast was two pieces of toast, one scalded egg, a half grapefruit and a cup of cocoa. Ms. James was not there as she left very early.

We left at ten, and not too far from the house we made a right turn at the bottom of the hill. That church was one mile up the hill. The school was right across the street from the church! So, five days for school and one for church and no way up there but on foot!

I thought more about that than almost anything else I had heard about the place. Puffing and blowing, I finally reached the church. The service was good and a well-known Presbyterian hymn was sung, "Behold the Mountain of the Lord." I like the tune very much even today.

Ms. T introduced me to everyone and the minister really gave me a warm welcome. Going down the hill was not that easy and often I had to grab for the wayside bushes to break my downward speed. Was I glad to get to the level and to the house! I was beat and so not ready for food. As I got to the room, I found May had fixed some lemonade for me. I was so grateful! I told her I was not hungry yet.

CHAPTER TWO: Jamaica

"We eat at two o'clock on Sundays. That's why Ms. James no stay ya pon Sunday. You must go wid her sometimes. She got friends roun dem parts. When she came she wen bring all kind of tings—cane, orange, grapefruit, banana, grata-cake and other tings, and she wen keep it right eena e box pon da shelf. She no gwine offer Ms. T one ting, but she gwine gie me and Cass sometin ef da even one piece a cane because we like eat cane."

Lunch was not bad at all and there was a small piece of bread pudding for dessert. We rested and had a quiet afternoon. After a cup of tea we went for a stroll. When we got back, Ms. James was there. She told me about her day and showed me what she had brought back. "You are welcome to anything. When you are going to school tomorrow take something with you."

Foremost in my mind was the daily uphill I had to do. "You'll get used to it in time and now and then you will get a lift," she said. I left it at that.

We went to bed early, got up early and set out at 8 o'clock for school at 9. I was to have over fifty children, five years old! But that would not be bad because the children would be very well behaved.

The day was really good and I liked the school. The challenge was to get the children ready for the Festival of Arts. There were no quarrels and Ms. T was doing fine.

One morning I heard Ms. James scraping out her corn-meal porridge. "Ah know you gwine eat it even when it half raw, she said.

I ate it because I would be hungry before noon and it was not going to kill me. I went to the kitchen and had a word with May. "You have to put on the porridge sooner so it is cooked through."

"Yea, Ms. V I really put it on too late." She was not vexed and I made up my mind to check on her so we could have a better life together.

Ms. James did not even wait for us. She picked up her things and went ahead. I just prayed that we would not begin the quarrels.

During the week I watched the children at lunch. May brought out our lunch in a carrier—lunch for three of us in a carrier! Anyway, we shared it with Ms. James walking away from it some days. She had her money and went to the shop for the extras.

But those dear little children rested heavily on my mind. Some came from three miles away with their school bag containing a brown paper bag and a bottle of something. I found out that they had something roasted—yam, coco, breadfruit, sweet potato, or a johnny-cake, and the bottle had cane juice, sugar and water, or lemonade. Some had a banana or other fruit. Some children had nothing and I discovered some had eaten their lunch before they got to school. Sometimes they brought a piece of cane. I was not in a position to help and my own lunch was often a problem to me.

I had to find ways to deal with the numbers in my class. There were three groups—the bright, the average and the dull and a few very dull, but they had to be worked in with the rest.

I had to work very hard making up individual slips for the bright ones. I numbered the slips so I started with #1 one day, #2 the next, and so on. They would get the work, but not in the same order and could work on their own books. If they got done before time they could borrow a book. Often I let them go outside with their books. I had asked a number of folk around to donate books—any kind—catalogues, magazines, storybooks, whatever, and it was interesting to observe what went on.

A catalogue was more fun with someone sharing it. I remembered what fun my brother and I had with a catalogue. We guessed what was on the next page—we guessed whether it would be men or women, boys or

CHAPTER TWO: Jamaica 49

girls. We looked for a figure we knew to see who found it first. To make the catalogues go round, I shared one in five pieces.

I got time to work with the "middlers" and played learning games. I made all kinds of flash cards -1 + 2 and if you had a 3 you hold it up and get a turn. Some days the A stream had things to do that were hard and then everybody got a chance at the books at the same time.

When they were going out to say the tables, I put them in groups. But the A's knew the tables and would lead off so the children were mixed up but able to help each other.

Words were fun times and I really liked the school. Then it happened. Ms. T was going out for most of the afternoon and she left me to mark the register. Now I protested, for when she was gone, Ms. James usually marked the register, she was the Assistant.

"I want you to do it today," she said and went out.

Ms. James was annoyed, so when the register was to be closed, nothing was done. I put out the books and the inks and pens and asked Ms. James to do it. I went to my class. I was only working as P and I knew well enough that in the absence of the Principal the Senior Assistant carried on.

Finally, Ms. James decided to do it. She was mad and in sitting down, she somehow caused the bottle of red ink to overturn. Wouldn't you know it! Right over the register page and on her dress! I ran for blotting paper, but the damage was done. I just knew we'd have fireworks when Ms. T got back.

Ms. T did not know what happened or how, but Ms. James' dress had the ink stain and the register was open so she went to her and pointed a finger at her. Ms. James pushed her away and they went at each other. We took the children outside and tried to go on with our work. Voices sounded louder, the blackboard fell down and I went in to see what was going on. It was serious so I ran upstairs for two teachers from the Home Economics Centre. They came down and parted the two, taking Ms. T upstairs with them.

Ms. James said she was leaving and told me that when I got home she would not be there. I begged her not to go, at least to sleep on it. We needed her as she knew how to get the children ready for the Festival. I could play the pieces but she held the key to the outcome. The children loved her and her way with them was fantastic. They had to take first place.

We were very sad because of what had taken place. Ms. T had to stop at the Manager's office to report the incident. She asked me to wait, but I wanted to get to the house to catch Ms. James.

When I got there, she had packed up and was ready to take the bus around five p.m. She was still angry and was crying. I joined her and we went into the room. I pleaded with her to stay. I wanted to get her away from the house which was depressing, so I suggested that she go visit two of the Primary School teachers up the street. If she still felt like it, she could go on the morning bus. I went with her.

The teachers were great and encouraged her to stay. They said she could spend the night with them and see how she felt in the morning. She agreed to do that. I went home. Ms. T came in and was very subdued. She could not even speak. I worried that I had got into her bad books. She saw Ms. James' things packed up as May and I had put them inside. Nobody wanted any supper. I went to my room and promptly dozed off. When I woke up it was almost seven p.m. so, not hearing Ms. T, I went to find her. I was sure she had gone to see Ms. Jones, one of the Primary School Teachers, about the day's events.

Ms. T said she had only asked me to do the register because she had a feeling that something bad was going to happen. She knew it was Ms. James' job. It was a bad place for me too but I really felt that Ms. T should not have asked me to do the work.

CHAPTER TWO: Jamaica

Ms. Jones told Ms. T that she should see Ms. James and apologize and maybe she'd stay. Ms. T said she was not going to. It was Ms. James' place to apologize to her.

"Well," said Ms. Jones dryly, "you have to consider the children and the Festival. We all know they are so good they will go to finals, but forget it if you lose Ms. James now. Where will you find another teacher? The school already has a reputation for losing good teachers and right now you have a good team.

"Go to see Ms. James and ask her to stay. You don't even have to apologize. Going to her will be enough."

We offered to go with her. She would never make it without our support. She did not say anything. She did not get up so we went to her and said, "Let's go."

We took about five minutes to get there and Ms. Jones, in her own very positive and powerful way, said,

"Ms. James, we are so glad you did not go away. Ms. T has something to say."

It was like death. Nothing felt alive to me, but I wanted Ms. James to stay. We had got on well together and she said she might even come back for another year. That meant no promotion for me. I would have moved into Ms. James' position, but I managed and the Education Officer had been pleased with what I had done. Ms. T said simply,

"Ms. James, I am here to ask you not to leave the school. I am sorry for what happened today."

All of us were crying and then Ms. James said she was sorry, too, and they shook hands. We all hugged each other. Ms. Martin said, "We have to celebrate." All they had was ginger ale so we got out glasses and celebrated with that.

Ms. James still spent the night with the others and Ms. T and I went home. We talked a little and I asked what made her not want Ms. James to do the register.

"I dreamt that she was marking it and the red ink turned over on the register."

"Let's go to bed," I said and that we did.

The next day we started all over. Our children won the local, the area, and went on to win the trophy for their performance of "Grasshopper Green" and "Callers." Ms. James really had that special touch that made children rise to the occasion. One would have to see and hear to understand it. She is one of those persons who should have been given the opportunity to work with music for the young. These were mostly poor, underfed children for whom music was part of the joy of life. As I looked at them and thought of those little brown bags, I knew their hungers were forgotten in the moments that gave them a touch of real joy.

Along Uncharted Ways

Summer holidays came and I knew that Ms. T and her sister were going to visit family in England. Where would I spend it? I would be getting my four pounds and I had saved twelve shillings. Ms. T said she was not going to charge me for the time as she knew Kingston was a hard place. I could stay there as May would be there to take care of the house and I did stay for a week.

Then I took a one-day trip to Kingston and met Major Slater of the Salvation Army Hostel.

She said, "Come along and we will have a good time together. I have a nice room for you."

From one window I could see the sea and from the other the goings on of a busy street. King Street was just around the corner as was the Kingston Parish Church that was open all day. I would pay seven shillings a week for the room and she would let me be in her area if I wished.

I made plans to return. I went back to Carron Hall, spent a few more days and then went to Kingston. May had told me I would be welcome back any time as she had to sleep at the house until Ms. T got back. She fixed me a nice box to take to town. I gave her five shillings and gave Cass two. All my clothes had been laundered.

CHAPTER TWO: *Jamaica*

May and I had struck a bargain shortly after I got there. I was doing my laundry when she came up and said,

"Ms. V, you neh mek fe hard work."

She took up a piece of clothing I had wrung out and showed me how much water I had left in it.

"See weh I tell you, mek a meh bargain wid you. You help Cass wid her lesson da evening time and we wan wash fe you. I noh busy right now, se mek a tek over dis washin right now."

She called Cass to get clothespins and sent her to hang out the clothes. That was a wonderful bargain. She told Cass that from next week I would help her with lessons. So, that was how she had my clothes ready. I did not have to take everything either, as she would take care of them.

I left for Kingston on Monday and found Major expecting me. I gave her the box of goodies May had packed, as food was not allowed in the room. She was grateful. I had tea with her that evening and we really hit it off.

I had to get a pair of shoes and some underwear and after looking at my cash, I saw that I could just manage until payday. I paid twenty-eight shillings for the month though it made a hole in what I had left after the money for May, Cass and bus fare was added to it. I had to buy food every day.

I felt a bit lonely, but I would make the best of it. Neither Ms. T nor I had talked about the A2 post she had promised me. Ms. James was not too sure what she would do, but I felt she would not return. I made up my mind to go back anyway. Ms. T was kind to me.

I went to the Salvation Army events as the Hall was just across the park and everything there was very interesting. Some nights I strolled around the areas where the groups were worshipping. The gowns, vestments, mitres, all were like any seen in liturgical churches, as well as singing, preaching, long prayers and plenty of clapping. Often a reader read a verse and then the preacher gave his interpretation. I discovered later that often the preachers could not read or else had bad eyesight.

Major had a good library and I did a lot of reading.

I had not told anyone where I was because I did not want anyone to know I was at the Salvation Army Hostel. Pride had taken over. So the end of the month came and they had nowhere to send my pay. Now, my cash was getting low. I sent May a note by the bus that took up Ms. James' clothing, but when I went back to see if she had sent my pay, there was no mail for me.

I began to reckon with pride for I was now getting down to crackers and cheese and lemonade. I went out every day. Some evenings Major invited me to share supper with her and we begged God to forgive me and straighten out things for me.

I got down to sixpence and went down to a little book-store that carried all kinds of interesting booklets. I had looked at one called *Science of Mind* that came from England. It was five pence. I paid Mr Goulette with sixpence and got my book and a penny. He asked if I did not want to subscribe to the magazine, but I told him I'd let him know after I read it. He told me how good it was and that I should read it and come in to chat about it sometime.

Well, I hurried to my room and found that I could not really understand the lead article written by the editor. I thought of borrowing ten shillings from Major but decided against that idea. Maybe my money would come later. Hopefully the next day.

So here I was with my penny. I decided to stay in my room and spend a quiet, prayerful morning. I was homesick but managed to put it away. On to noon, I was on my knees, just there as it were without words, but in an attitude of trust.

I heard footsteps on the stairs and the person was coming down the hall. There was a rap at my door. I asked

CHAPTER TWO: Jamaica

who it was. "It's me, Rhoda, mam. Today is my father's birthday and my mother would like you to have lunch with us." I thanked her and said I'd be down shortly.

The janitor and his wife had been friendly and helpful. She did my laundry and would take no money. I sat in their quarters in the evenings when I did not go to the Hall or was not otherwise occupied. We talked about many things and he was interested in travel, talking about all the places in Jamaica where he lived as a railway worker. He liked to read so he could discuss the pros and cons of articles he'd read in the *Readers' Digest*. He was a very interesting man, but now he was not vey well. She was beautiful, soft spoken, hard working and had a touch that was strange because of its great warmth. Rhoda, at eighteen was the youngest of five. All the others were living elsewhere. Rhoda worked at a store on Princess Street.

I went to say hello to them when I first went to the Hostel and his wife said to me, "How are you going to get your clothes washed?"

I said, "I don't know."

"Let me tell you something, to make it easy, just bring down your clothes and I will wash them. I know you are not at home and you must miss your home. This place doesn't have an adequate place for you to do your washing."

So, for the time I was there, she did my laundry and would not take anything for it. I intended to give her some money when I got my cash.

So, I was upstairs crying when Rhoda came knocking at my door saying,

"Mommy says we ready to eat now."

Then she saw me and said, "Oh, Lord, you can't be homesick for Daddy's birthday."

The lady had cooked a lot and had the table fixed so nice. But I could not eat one bite. So she had Rhoda carry my dinner to my room. I sat there in my room and ate and ate. How God acts in those situations! He knew I needed a person like her and that special food. You cannot buy that. That was very enlightening to see how those people would deal with me even though they did not know me. They just had a feeling, God put it so.

That was a very interesting period. Every day I went out and stayed out all day. In the mornings I went to the shop where a lot of working people went. I bought a piece of cheese and a biscuit. I took my cup, bought lime and sugar and asked for water to make limeade. And I sat on the park bench and was well satisfied. Then I started walking around the town. At 12 o'clock I went to the parish church and said prayers there.

But I did not have anything to do and nowhere to go, so I decided to observe how the poorer people made their living. I went down to the market and talked with people to see how all of them manage. It was quite an education! Lots of time the talk was so sweet between the two of us, I ended up with a piece of their candy. One day a girl said,

"Miss, do you want to try it out here? I just need to go to the shop. Can you mind my stall for me?"

I managed all right and she came back soon.

Each day, as I looked through my window at the Salvation Army hostel, I was fascinated by the events that took place. In the midst of what seemed like a rapidly boiling pot, there was laughter and tears, anger and peace, pain and anxiety, and language that sounded like all the echoes of man's inhumanity to man coming to a centering.

I visited the shops and stores; the street venders were interesting. I spent a lot of time at the Crafts Market and now and then I took a tram ride so I could see all around. What a place this Kingston was. I was fascinated by it.

Everywhere there was the great hunger for better than the dehumanizing and demoralizing existence in which so many were forced to live. Or, on second thoughts, how many did not have to live that way? This experience triggered something in me and I wrote a long poem. Here is one verse.

I heard a burdened woman sigh
I saw a lonely woman cry
I wondered if they knew God nigh
And how it was to die.

I wondered about the Christian Gospel and the meaning of the Faith after the almost two thousand years of liberty of Christ. What was that? Why did people have to live like that? By far the "have not" people seemed like a hundred times the "haves." In our concept of God's love, where were we hoarding our share? Even me, with my few shillings, what was I failing to do, or better, to be?

There are all kinds of poor: the poor in spirit, the primary poor, secondary poor, and the rich-poor who knew not that they were poor. How is it that we think that we come to terms with God and yet forget all about the poor? Life is so total. As the Bible says, the sparrow's fall and the number of hairs of a man's head are important.

Deep, deep in the very core of my being I heard words—important words from the Bible—I heard Malachi's "Wherein have we?"

I heard Amos and his talk about the rich who prospered and only remembered themselves; of those lying on expensive beds and couches, of the winter house, the summerhouse and the great house! I heard Solomon and his words that God should give neither poverty nor riches, and his clear reasons for that. I heard Jesus and the statement about the widow's mite. When all the offerings together were put against it, hers was of more value because she had given her all, including herself, and so her sacrifice. What did my giving cost me most of the time? God, I thought, just when are we going to learn what giving to you really means?

And the poor? Jesus himself said; "Happy are the poor!" That was some statement—happy and poor—

how can one reconcile them? It had to mean a certain kind of poorness, a state of not being self sufficient so that the sufficiency was of God. Then we come to a state of having, as Paul said: "nothing, yet possessing all things." What a great idea!

What I began to see as I considered the poor was about wants and needs and that our responsibility for each other had to do with needs and not wants. If in any way we prevent or deny to another their needs in so far as we are able to share, then we are a hindrance, for it is no use to think that we give to Him while failing to consider the needs of each other. It is in living with more than our own needs that we begin to feel that we have no needs and we deny God.

Primary poverty seems to mean having nothing and having no way of getting needs met. Secondary poverty means having a little and always wanting more and more and never living out of debt because of trying to meet wants. Then the real poor are the haves who have no need to think about anyone else's needs.

The matter of the poor continued to be foremost in my mind for a few days and then I decided to get close to this kind of poor. I took a walk to the west and with my change purse tightly held with my souvenir penny. I did not feel hungry at all, for somehow I was not thinking about food. I was wholly encompassed by the poor. I went to one of the tenement housing areas past the May Pen cemetery and started to talk with people.

They all wanted to know what my business was, and most of them thought that I had really come to look for them for the welfare or for politics or for the church, but not just to visit. They were all very nice to me, but only one or two allowed me inside.

As I went along I got very thirsty for it was a very hot day, so I spoke to a woman who was cooking outside. She offered me a seat on a box and I asked her for a drink of water. She was sorry that she did not have a

CHAPTER TWO: Jamaica

glass, but she washed out a 12-ounce jam bottle and went to the pipe for the water. It was just about ten feet to the pipe and I had a queer feeling to think that I had to drink out of a jam bottle. It was clean for I saw her wash it out well, but I was beginning to experience the feel of the "have" as against the "have not." That kind woman told me to rest as long as I wanted to, but I went on with the visiting. They could not understand me being there on my own. Neither could I.

As I went on, I came to a man feeding his scrawny pigs. He was quite civil and invited me inside where his lady was ironing. We had a good chat as she took trips outside to watch her pot. I offered to do a little ironing but she turned me down with a laugh. I guess that I looked like someone who would surely scorch her clothes. I may have, too, for I had not done much ironing of starched clothes. I heard that man was a fisherman and that he did not believe in God because, if there was a God, he would not have to punish like he was.

Now this man had just about the best kept place of those that I had seen. It was clean, had good furniture, curtains and plastic flowers on the little centre table. I could not see into the bedroom for he had fixed a partition and there was a hardboard door. Except for the smell of pigs so close to the house, and the chickens around, it was in good shape. But here he was blaming God for not supplying his wants. While we were inside talking, she was outside with her cooking. As I got to the back door through which I had entered, she said she had just fixed something to offer me. She had the plate in her hand and asked me if I would stay and have it. I almost said no, then changed my mind and accepted it. There was no table and she put the plate on a tray and passed me a spoon. It was a regular Jamaican boil-up with fish. I asked them if they were not going to eat too, but they were not ready so I sat there, ready to cry and had a good meal.

Afterwards she brought me a glass of iced red lemonade, which I found most refreshing. She had a cabinet with crockery so I did not have a jam jar this time. The man's name was Marcus and he made me promise that I would come again. So I did, after thanking them for their hospitality. As I walked away from the house she came running after me with a paper package containing a few oranges and four ripe bananas.

She was beaming and I could see that my being in their home and accepting what they offered had done something for them both. It had done a great deal for me also. It was a long walk back, much longer than it had seemed to get there, but I faintly got home and took to bed. I was tired to the bone, but I was happy. I shared the fruit with the Major and she invited me to a snack, but I told her that I would rather have it in the morning.

So ended that day. I had learned a few things about the poor and I had now given myself a whole lot of home-work to do about poverty. It was something I could not forget about very easily.

Sometimes I looked through my south window. Over the house tops and beyond was the sea, about one-quarter of a mile away. The beautiful blue-green sea was so soothing to me. I thought of my home and wonderful sea-shores and the summers spent at Mullins River which was truly a little paradise.

I am never truly happy away from the sea, for it seems to be built into the fibre of my being. I can stay away from it for so long and then there comes the haunting of some missing factor. A little time by water anywhere helps, but there is nothing like the smell of the sea air and the simple knowing that the water is there.

I looked on the roof tops and wondered what went on inside the tenements. The ones I knew of were overcrowded and most of them had a lot of hostile, overprotective people. So many people lived on the edge of nowhere and nobody was satisfied with anything really. It was sharing of space, which belonged to none of them. Children had nowhere to play, no home life at all and they were absorbing the distress of the adults. To walk into a tenement yard was quite an experience indeed. Babies were never lacking. Some were sick—runny-nosed, hair uncombed, clean, dirty, nappie-less, pants-less, crying, whining, itchy, but some were healthy, laughing, friendly babies looking out on life through beautiful eyes, crawling and falling off and hurting and getting spanked for they know not what. Babies loved and unloved, so many with mother love alone. Babies and babies and babies.

What did they have for food? Sugar and water, cornmeal pap with sugar, a few were breast-fed, but so many grow up on condensed milk. God's babies, but without doubt babies born of the will of man, babies born of the flesh and some babies born of the will of God and out of them all were those gems of purest ray, serene. Sometimes in the lack of understanding of life where there is a sowing and a reaping, one is tempted to say,

"Great Father, why does this continue for so long?"

And out of the folly of the question is the answer,

"My ways are not your ways, neither are my thoughts your thoughts."

That has served me for a long, long time.

When I get quiet, the pressure of people comes in, and I have to spend a lot of time asking what they need and how I can help. I feel this more at night, but I have learned how to handle it. If a spirit seeks help, I must try to help and God has ways we do not understand.

Making Connections

One day Major Slater said; "Major Wilson has invited us to come over to the men's side for tea."

We went over there for tea and were talking about British Honduras. In came the Major's two children so he asked why they came home so early.

"We told the teacher we would like to go early because we want to be there for this teacher from British Honduras. The teacher asked us who the visitor was and we told her,

"Miss Vernon from British Honduras. She is at the hostel with Major Slater and Daddy and Mommy invited Major and Miss Vernon to tea, so we want to be there."

The two children questioned me about British Honduras and we had such a nice time. Then the children told me, "The music teacher says she is sure she knows you because a lady by the name of Miss Vernon stayed at her house one night on her way to Trinidad."

After the tea the children were excited to tell the music teacher. And I was excited to see how God would link us up. Two days ago I was left with a penny. Then I had been invited to lunch and now to tea. Yes, the daily bread was being provided. I had not gone back to the bus, as that seemed to be a hopeless venture.

When the Major and I got home, the telephone rang and here was the music teacher saying;

"What are you doing there? How long have you been there?"

"A couple of weeks," I answered.

"Well, put your things together and tomorrow at four o'clock, Ronald will be coming to pick you up. You will come to our house to stay."

After hanging up, I told Major that I would be leaving and I would be with the music teacher the children spoke of. She was glad for me, but said she would miss me. I thanked her and went to put my things together. As I left, she gave me an envelope.

CHAPTER TWO: Jamaica

Major Slater knew them too but she said; "I never knew that you knew them."

"I only met them one night when I was in transit." I told her.

That is how I got to the big Soutar house at 95 East Street. A. Dudley Soutar was Assistant to the Prime Minister, his brother was Clerk of the Legislative Council and his sister taught music, both private lessons at home and at Kingston College for Boys—a very important family. Ronald was their driver and they had several other servants. So I moved from my quarters at the Salvation Army into the Soutar house with seventeen rooms. I had made a transition into a different world altogether. From then on I always stayed with the Soutars whenever I was in Kingston.

I was told that all that was being asked of me was to help around and to help with the Daughters of the King, a girls' organization at St. George's Church. I had many skills and taught the girls to do tatting, crochet, drawn thread work and hardanger.

I still did not have more than my penny but I was rich. It would be three weeks before I would be back in Carron Hall. Then, as I got ready for bed, I remembered the envelope Major had given me. I opened it and she had given me ten shillings and a note saying; "Come again and please keep in touch."

My friend Ernestine was the Soutars' aunt. She lived in her little quarters in the back section of the house. I had visited her when I was living with my great-aunt, but I always went in the back gate and never had anything to do with the rest of the family, so they did not even know I was there.

I went back to work to find Ms. James had decided not to return. I got my promotion after all. Things were working well for I had my paycheck to start out with.

Appendicitis

I only stayed at Carron Hall for nine months that year because I was stricken with an attack of appendicitis. Two men carried me down the hill sitting in their arms. I went to Kingston the next day and saw the doctor who said the appendix had to come out right away. But I had no money or family. What was I to do? I was staying with the Soutar family who cooked for Arch Dean Ramson. The maids were to take his tea to him in a basket, but Jamaicans do not like to carry baskets so they left it right there. But I was from British Honduras and did not mind. I saw the basket sitting there and thought he must be hungry so I took it over. He noticed my strange accent and asked me why I was there, so I told him about my appendix. He wanted to know where I would go and I said I did not know. He told me not to worry that he would take care of it. He called Dr. Wilson James at the Nuttall Hospital and arranged everything. That was a big money hospital.

"How are you going to pay Dr. James?" he said, and then he laughed. "Don't worry about it, your doctor and your hospital are OK."

So I went to Nuttall Hospital and had one of the best surgeons do my surgery. I did not pay any money because I carried that tea over on time and he appreciated it. No one told me to do it. I just knew that church was over and he must be hungry. You see how those things pay off. I was not looking for any reward. I did it just for kindness. When people think I am stupid for doing certain things, I leave them right there in their folly. God gives his reward in his own way when you do the right thing in a good spirit.

So, I entered the hospital for what was to be a simple operation. I remember getting the anaesthetic that sent me whirling through a dark, horizontal tunnel and coming to an explosion of bright light bursting all around and then nothing more.

CHAPTER TWO: Jamaica

Later I learned that I was in that theatre for many hours because of cardiac arrest. Instead of the expected two days, I spent eighteen days looking like all my blood had gone and feeling a weakness that frightened me. I could not move. I could only blink my eye. As I looked back at myself lying there unable to move at all but able to use the mind, I was grateful for all that I had learned as an Anglican. It was really the prayers, the psalms, the hymns, and their deep religious impact on my life that held me in good stead all those days. I did not really think of death at all, though I realized that I was very ill. There was no I.V., no signs around me that I was as ill as I was. There was not even a memory of the doctor coming in, but this was a private hospital and he would not spend much time there. If necessary, he would have to be called. In some ways, the aloneness was good therapy and I realize that even now when I am ill, I just want to be left alone. When I am ready, I will take food, but my body makes rapid recovery in silence.

Some of the nurses learned that I read tea leaves. They insisted that I do readings for them in the hospital. Every day they would put their teacups in the locker by my bed for me to read and then I would read the teacup. I do not see anything in the cup. The cup is just a medium. It is a knowing that is beyond the tea leaf. Sometimes I could not tell them anything. I remember one lady who was very sick and the hospital was very expensive. She wanted her husband to go to the States because he could make money there. I saw a boat in her tea leaves and told her that he would go. That is what actually happened.

When I was well enough to leave the hospital, the Archdeacon arranged for me to spend two weeks at a convalescent home in the St. Andrews Hills. I began to feel strong again but knew that there would be no more hill climbing at Carron Hall. I had to find a new job. Someone must need me.

The Lonely Place

After I recovered from my appendectomy, Ruby Meredith from the Education Office asked me to teach her brother's children. They lived in a secluded place in the interior of Portland where there was no school. The offer sounded good. I would not be a governess, but a tutor. I accepted, little knowing what I was letting myself into.

At the end of a long bus journey, I was met by a woman and a boy, who helped me with my luggage. Traveling light becomes a feature of those who must move about. The externals have to be light, but the internals—their weight cannot be measured.

We went down a narrow, winding path and came to a river to be crossed by a log!

"Oh Lord," I thought.

The boy went over sideways with the suitcase. He came back for a basket and a small box, and then we crossed. I was very nervous, but I was at one of those points from which there was no turning back. The boy made his second trip and waited, for he was needed to help us from the end of the log to the land.

All of a sudden, I was homesick, but I set out and crossed as the boy had done. The woman came last. She said,

"Thank God we got over."

But the journey to the house was still a quarter of a mile away, round and round going up the hill. Why did not anyone tell me this? Life is often like that. If we knew, we would never venture into what often turns out to be needed experience for our journey.

Finally, the journey ended at the hilltop and the little family seemed genuinely excited to see me. The children, four, six, and eight, were delighted, all coming around and trying to stake their claim. It ended up with the little one getting a side to herself and the other two sharing the other side. They were well-trained,

CHAPTER TWO: Jamaica

delightful children and I began to feel my place with them.

We all had supper, simple and wholesome, and as the children had been up past bedtime, they had to go to bed. The parents and I talked about what they wanted me to do and we all went to bed. I got very little sleep, for the room, though large and airy, smelled of the bats that flew in and out. Thank goodness I had a net!

Next morning all the children said they took a long time to fall asleep. They were still excited and happy that I had come. They volunteered to help me put away my things and the youngest was rather surprised at how little I had.

"Are the rest of your things coming on the bus?" she queried.

"This is all I have." I said.

She looked at the extent of my things.

"This is all she has," she told the other two. They had no comment. Then, as an afterthought, the older one said, "Well, up here we do not have anywhere to go anyway."

I had a few books, which they set neatly on the table. In the suitcase were three books with their names written in them. Well, what a thing these children had!

"She brought us presents!" Thank you, with a kiss. They immediately forgot about helping me put things away. They went off to show their presents to Mom and Dad.

I put away my things in a chest of drawers and hung up my dresses on one of these open hanging places that had pretty cretonne in front. I had a pair of slippers and two pairs of shoes, which were put on the floor where my dresses were hung.

There were plenty of citrus fruits and also as much cow's milk as we wanted. This family was not poor, but they were not wealthy either, yet they were happy.

With someone to tutor their children they were really at ease. After breakfast there was the important family devotion. This was a new procedure in family life for me. I had my own personal devotions and in my growing up family each had, too, but this was new and refreshing.

The little room set aside for school was comfortable. The necessities were there and lessons went very well.

Altogether, except for some loneliness, mainly due to the sameness, the experience was good. There was a road behind the property that led to a small town. The maid and the boy often went there, but walking the two miles up and down and around the town was too much for me.

After five months there, the father found a job in Kingston, and we prepared to move. All our things would go by road through the town. We would cross the log and someone with a car would take us to the new place. The children made a big ceremony on leaving the house and they all hoped they would never have to go back there. It was a lonely place.

They begged me to stay with them for awhile anyway. Where I stayed in Kingston was very near to where they would be, so I promised to continue with the children as this was in the middle of the term.

A New Friend

In Kingston the children settled down quickly and I worked at preparing them for their classes in school. They had grown up with governesses and tutors and they had all sorts of dreadful feelings about school.

This time I made friends in Kingston. One night my friend Jean and I attended a party some distance away from where we lived. There was very little transport in those days and buses did not run after eleven o'clock. We felt it was not such a bad walk, so we trudged up to the home and decided to take the last bus back. We had a good time and left in time, or so we thought, for

CHAPTER TWO: Jamaica

the last bus. But we did not make it and decided to walk home.

There were lots of tales going around about soldiers who molested people on the streets, but as we were not that far away and there were two of us, we took a chance. Furthermore, Jean and I had agreed that she would phone the house when she thought I had got home. There was only one doubt in my mind. After my friend got to her street I still had to cross a gully and the racecourse, before I would be on my street that was sure to have a few people around.

Jean reached her street and ran home, and I decided to go for it. I had not gone very far when I heard footsteps behind me. When I walked fast, whoever it was did the same and to make it worse, it seemed to be two soldiers. Maybe they knew I was afraid and were teasing me. I started to sweat, and to get very tired, and began to plan what I would do. I was on a street where all the fences had these gates that formed part of the fence, and if you did not know where to look for the string, you would not readily know where the gate was. I recognized one of the gates ahead and as I got to it, I pulled the string and went inside hoping there were no dogs. The footsteps went right past the gate.

As I got inside the gate, I heard a voice saying, "Good night," coming from a kitchen with the back along the fence.

"I just came in to hide from the soldiers," I said.

That was enough. I heard how lucky I was and tales of what had happened to people around the racecourse.

"You can't go home now," she said, "You can call your folks and let them know where you are and that you will come home early in the morning."

I knew that the senior member of the household would be awake decoding war telegrams, so I called as she suggested. They were already worrying after the last bus had come and gone down. Since no one was available to come for me, they agreed that I should stay where I was if I thought it was all right. I said I felt OK about it.

She introduced herself as "Miss Leah" and said that she hardly went to bed before one and that she was just taking a little smoke in the cool. She offered me a seat and said that she would fix a bed for me. After her smoke and a chat with me, she went upstairs and in a short while she called to me to come up.

She apologized for not lending me a nightie, but said it would "swallow me up". I told her I would be quite all right in my slip, and it would soon be morning anyway. She went down and I closed the doors. There were no lights and no key to the door. But if she locked the door at the bottom of the steps, no one could get upstairs. I took off my shoes and my dress and lay on the bed thinking.

I was uneasy. My twenty-three years felt like twelve, for I needed mother, grandmother, uncles, protection. "God, please help me," I said, and tried to quiet my fears.

Then I heard someone coming up the stairs. Maybe it was Miss Leah going to bed. The steps were not hers, though, for she had on soft shoes. Then I heard the knob to the door so I asked who was there. A man's voice answered. I told him he had the wrong room, but he just opened the door and came in. I was already half off the bed and started to put on my dress. I wondered whether to scream or to fight but I decided that if Leah was part of this, that would do me no good. Long ago an older friend had taught me what has stood me in good stead in many an emergency. "Still your mind and ask God to quicken your wits." I did just that.

He went around to the other side of the bed and took off his shoes, shirt and pants. I sat on the chair. He got in the bed and told me to get in with him. I stayed where I was. He suggested that he could easily put me down but he did not want to do that. I then told him I was there by accident and before I could say any more, he said,

Chapter Two: Jamaica

"You have an accent. Where are you from?"

"Guess," I answered.

He tried and failed, but I did not tell him. That was enough to give me a chance.

"Lie down, Miss," he said, "let us talk some more."

Slowly I got up and did as he asked. He made no attempt to touch me.

"Relax. You are trembling. Lie down, Miss," he said again, as I raised up. ""What are you doing here?"

I told him the story and he had quite a few bad words in store for Miss Leah.

"I believe you and I am not going to do you anything. I could not hurt you even if I wanted to." He wanted to talk some more. He took a while and then he said,

"It is funny, but I feel like you are my sister. I never felt like that before."

I asked him what he was doing there and he told me all about his work and his life. He was an electrician and climbed poles to fix lights. He did not smoke or drink, but he liked women and spent a lot of time in brothels. He was young and fair and handsome and single. His speech told me that his education was not that good, but I could sense that he was thinking. He offered to take me home, but I said that I would stay until daylight. He wanted to know my address so he could visit me. I told him I would have to clear the matter, but before he left, I wrote down the telephone number for him.

"Let me hold your hands a little," he said, "because I have never met someone like you."

There was something about this stranger that made me think very hard. What was it? He held my hands and after a while he got up and put on his clothes. Then he started to tell me everything he was going to tell Miss Leah. I got up as he went down the stairs, but there was no Miss Leah, so he went through the gate.

I put on my dress, put the chair on the veranda and sat looking at the sky. I was tired, but all I could do was wait for the morning. At the break of day, I eased out of the yard and went home.

Later I told Ernestine what had taken place. She thought it was a good idea to let him visit because she wanted to have a look at him. It was not many days later when he phoned and asked me to go to a movie with him. I told him that he could come to the house, but I would not go to the show. He came looking like a real gentleman. He was a bit shy, but Ernestine put him at ease and soon he was telling her about himself. He did not stay very long and she invited him to come again.

In telling us about his work, he mentioned how dangerous it was to climb a pole. A little thing could cause you to fall or be shocked so he tried to be extra careful. After several visits, he arrived one evening with a paper package saying it was for all of us. It was ice cream and we sat around the table and chatted. All in the family seemed to like him. Then we sat on a bench in the garden and he said he had something to tell me. He told me that he had changed.

"From the night I met you at Miss Leah's, I have never been there again. In fact, I have not been elsewhere either. I have not even gone to a show."

He said that even his mother and grandmother had spoken about his change, and there was only one thing they wanted him to do—go to church—and that he was planning to go. He was a Catholic, but he had not been to church for a long time. He asked about my church and said that maybe we could go together sometime. It remains one of my regrets that I did not see that as an important sign. There was no reason for not asking him to go that next Sunday. I was shy but felt that when we knew each other better, I would invite him.

Ernestine was interested in the fact that he spoke about going to church. She told me that when he came again, I should ask him and she would go along with us. When he came in the evening, he told us that he had gone to his own church.

One morning, Alva Boland came in to me with the paper in her hand. "Isn't this the young man that has been coming here?"

It was. He had been working on a pole and had been electrocuted! We were all sad, but I had not really entered into an emotional relationship with him yet. I thought about it and concluded that we had enjoyed all that was meant for us, and that our lives had crossed for that short period so he might begin his new life on earth and leave it with his mind turned God-ward.

The old lady was shaken. "Such a nice man," she said, "but God had it all worked out for him to meet you just the way it happened. God was behind it all, child. Don't feel bad. It is God's doing."

I was stunned, too. I had lost a friend, a very special kind of friend. What I thought of most was Miss Leah and how beyond her scheming she had been used by God as an instrument for his purposes to be filled. I tried to find her place, but never did. I could not tell which gate was hers because all had a high wooden fences with strings hanging out.

Time and again I thought of that night and know that the spirit of the Lord is in every place. I learned how important it is not to make hasty decisions about people, but to slow down the process, to give the benefit of the doubt and not to write people off.

The Old Servant

It was a hot, sultry day and by early afternoon I could do nothing besides getting in bed for awhile. As I lay there, I saw as though one of the old servants came in with a brown envelope and a bankbook.

She said, "I want to take the weekend off and would like you to keep these for me. This is my Penny Bank book and in this envelope is my will and my sister's address."

I came to myself and there was no servant, no bankbook, no envelope. I did not say anything to anyone but my thoughts were very deep. I got up and went downstairs and watched that old servant as she went about her duties. She had a room not very far away. I had been there many times when she had her weekends off. She had a very hard bed with a thin horsehair mattress. There were all her little "coutrements", as she called her things. There was an old trunk in which she kept a pair of sheets, pillowcases, a white spread and two towels, two nighties, and two panties. I knew what these were for. She used to laugh and tell me if anything happened to her, I was the only one to go in the trunk. She did not want to be buried in Kingston, but on the family property where her sister lived.

She liked for me to take a rest on her bed so when she knew I was coming, she fixed up the room and always fixed up a lunch, which we had together. There was no space at the table for two, but she insisted that I sit there while she sat with her plate on her lap. She smoked tobacco and the room had the smell just as all her clothes did. She could only see out of one eye as the other was what people called a "fish eye", one where the pupil is white. She was a good house cleaner and kept the floors of the house shining bright.

There was not much to life for her, but she was very fond of me. When I got into a chat with her, she recounted her life in Port Limon where her parents had migrated in one of the many migrations of Jamaicans to Panama, Costa Rica, and other places. She had one child, a son, but they got separated somehow and she never found where he went. He was supposed to have gone on a ship.

Her bed was very hard, but it made her happy for me to be there. I felt quite happy to be there too. I never told anyone at our house where I went on those days.

Chapter Two: Jamaica

As I was preparing for bed on the day I had the vision of her, I heard a rap and said, "Come," for I knew her footsteps. Here she was with her envelope and her Penny Bank book! Both were entrusted to my care. Early in the morning she planned to take the bus and go to see her sister. She would return on Monday and come to work on Tuesday. She returned and I got her belongings to give to her. She suggested that I keep them, but I told her she should give them to her employer and tell him her wishes. She did.

On Wednesday morning as I was leaving for school, I noticed that she was not around, so I went to her room and found her sitting on the floor. She liked to sit on the floor, but I was very uneasy because I encouraged her to get up and she made no effort. She was all right and would soon get up, she told me.

I was teaching and, as it was time to leave, I went out, but asked the other two maids to check on her. When I returned at 2:30 p.m., she was just where I had left her. The others had given her something to eat, but she only took some coffee. It was serious. I called the others to help and it took four of us to put her in the bed.

I cleaned her up and by this time realized that she had suffered a stroke and the lower half of her body was affected. She was quite conscious, but weak. I called her employer and suggested that he ask the doctor to come. I would be there.

The family doctor came and said she needed to be in the hospital, so he called for the ambulance and I got her ready to go. I talked with her about it and she started to cry, but I promised to go with her and promised that she would be taken care of. Her employer had come by this time and he promised to let her sister know.

The ambulance came and I went with her for I knew she was frightened as well as worried, and the most one could do was to continue to be a friend. Her sister came, but she could not stay for long, and we promised to keep her aware of events.

I knew my friend did not have long to be here for she also had diabetes. I sensed that she, too, knew that this world was not her home. She grew quieter and one evening when I went, she had lapsed into unconsciousness and she passed away in the early morning hours.

I had prayed with her and for her and I felt badly that she had to die, as it were, alone. Her sister came back, but she had already passed away. She was satisfied that we had done what we could. Arrangements were made for the body to be taken to her family home where she was buried.

My friend did not have much to make her happy. As long as she could work and keep those floors shining, she felt worthwhile. On the cook's day off, she looked after the meals and she enjoyed doing that.

She was illiterate and wanted no one to know it and I never found out how she communicated with her sister before I came to live there, but she trusted me. I wrote her letters for her and read to her what he sister said when she wrote back.

Her sister came later and cleared up the room, but for the final rest, I told her she should take the things her sister had prepared for such a time. We went to the house and put the sheets, pillowcases, spread, towels, soap, stockings, powder, and a little money wrapped in a bit of brown paper. Those she carried away. After the funeral she made one trip and did away with the rest of the things.

For me, there was sadness that I could not explain to anyone. It was the loss of a kindred spirit that only the other knows what is left. There is, however, a real sense of thankfulness for the time the Great Planner of our lives allowed us to journey together.

The Trusting Child

I had a friend whose baby was very ill. She had gastroenteritis and nothing seemed to be helping. The baby seemed to be dying. Then another friend came with an idea. Get a clean white bottle and fill it with water. Take it to the healing temple in Jonestown get it blessed in the night service and then bathe the baby in it. This sounded like something I should not miss, so I volunteered to go.

I found the place, put my bottle of water in a designated spot. There were circles of bottles leading to a single at the top. There was a lot of singing and marching around the bottles. Only certain ones marched around. They faced the north, south, east, west, and with each point there were specifics—the Lord's Prayer, the Twenty-third Psalm, the Apostles Creed, the Doxology. There were prayers at each step. When the service was over, you took your bottle quietly and went home.

I hurried to my friend. The one who told her about it was waiting, too. They poured out the water in a basin and nervously put the baby in. They poured the water over the head, making sure that every part of the body was washed. It was a kind of baptism. Then they dried the baby and lovingly, tenderly put her in her crib. There was such as stillness, a trustful waiting. The baby was resting, but not looking much better.

We all went to sleep. Very early the next morning the baby's mother called me. I thought the baby had passed on, but her face was saying something else. "Come!" was all she said. There was that baby standing up in her crib. She was weak, but she was strong enough to stand up holding on. We were all crying tears of joy—we had no words, no words at all. Joy had really come to us in the morning, and we praised God for His ways that are past finding out. I have often wondered what happened to a place like that. I tried to find it many years later, but progress demanded its space.

I have no harsh words for these people who, in absolute faith, prayed and trusted God in the way they felt called to do. There were too many people there with their bottles of water and their faith for me to believe that ours was the only answered prayer that night.

The establishment cries ignorance, and finds intolerant attitudes when these folk do the way they do—ways that are so unacceptable to the sophisticated, but it is always good to remember, "Go wash in the Pool of Siloam." And the way that Bible story it told.

How many might find a healing if the voice of the trusting child in them could be heard?

It was the story of Naaman—go, do what seems out of the ordinary, go take the water and see what I will do for you. All those bottles of water, all those people searching for healing for themselves and for others, and those who felt called to this kind of healing ministry! It was without money and without price—free giving of what God had given to that man and who, as he felt led, carried on that ministry for years.

Another Transition

I was still tutoring the children when one evening, the family was having company and I was asked to read their tea leaves. When I came to the cup for the children's dad, all I knew was that he was going away soon, by boat. He was getting a new job and he would go first, then we would come later. He noticed the "we". Yes, I was sure of it, I was going, too! He did not know of any such job.

Three weeks later he came in with a letter. He was asked to go to East Harbour, Turks and Caicos Islands. He would need to take a tutor for his children. As I learned later, it was not that there was no school, but no private school.

All my friends discouraged me from going. They called it a "hard time place", saying that all the time there was a water problem and food was hard to get sometimes. But people were living there, so I thought it could not be that bad. I was already conditioned to going, so there was no "discouragement that would make me relent once my avowed interest was to be a pilgrim," (adapted from *Monk's Gate* by J. Bunyan). So it was, he took the job, went to see how things were and to arrange for us. We went forty days after he left, and that is how I got to Turks and Caicos Islands.

I moved to East Harbour on South Caicos, a small island in the Turks Caicos chain, with Ruby Meredith's brother and his family. The family stayed for two years and I lived with them. I was paying back Ruby Meredith for all her kindnesses to me. I worked for the Y teaching handiwork. We got good sales for our things. It was a blessing, for the land was too salty to grown anything.

CHAPTER THREE
Turks and Caicos Islands (1944-49)

Living in East Harbour on South Caicos, a small island in the Turks Caicos chain, for five years was both a milestone and a jumping off place because I could read and concentrate without interruptions. It was so good to climb on the rocks, find a shady spot and enjoy a kind of privilege I have often yearned for. My mind wanted to dwell on religion and science, but I did not have the language to develop the thoughts and feelings in specific ways.

When they left, I boarded with another family and became Principal for the government primary school. I stayed another three years. Nobody from South Caicos had gone to high school in Grand Turk. The scholarships were always given to children from Grand Turk. I had five children ready to sit for the Grand Turk scholarship examination. It took some persuasion to get the parents to go to Grand Turk with their children so they could sit for the examination. Four of the parents could go and all five children passed. Two of the girls ended up as nurses and I took one boy with me to Jamaica. I hoped to get him an exceptional scholarship at Excelsior High School where I knew the Principal.

Solitude and Sweet Potations

What a place! Six hundred people, not much soil or water, plenty of places for salt-making, no fresh vegetables, bony fish and conch in abundance, beef or pork irregularly, chicken always available (as most people had their own), a resident doctor, a dentist for all the islands, three churches with no resident pastor, a midwife, a primary school with eight grades, three teachers and one hundred and forty-four children in the school.

Things were bad, very bad, on South Caicos, what with all the spoiled fruit and vegetables the Haitian boats brought, having been caught in a storm and then in a calm. There was no variety in diet—pear bush soup made from Turks Head cactus bud (a good okra substitute), cornmeal, dried conch soaked overnight, boney fish, very little drinking water and no sign of rain. We sat around the table and I said,

"I would love to get some sweet potatoes." It was just a joke and we all laughed. The two children made wishes for rice and stewed beans. Forget it! We went to bed.

Early the next morning there was someone at the door. It was an old lady looking for me so I went to the door. She had come from North Caicos and a friend who lived there asked her to give me a paper sack with something. I took it and peeked in. There were five small sweet potatoes she had sent for me. I thanked her for bringing it.

"Sweet potatoes," I called out, ""five—one for each of us—sweet potatoes!"

As it was too early to get up I went back to my room and reflected on the night before and on the timing. I found this Bible verse to be true—"Before they call, I will answer and while they are yet speaking, I will hear." It is true, true, true, in small things as in great. We only need to experience it once and for all.

A Baby Saved

One evening three children came knocking at my door carrying a baby and calling, "Teacher, teacher."

I took one look at the baby and felt that they should be at the nurse's door, not mine. I took the baby and saw that convulsions seemed close.

"Where is your mother?" I asked.

"At a meeting," they said, so I told the oldest to go for her.

No place was far away, but I felt that every minute meant more trouble and what if that baby died in my arms! I remembered the prayer.

"Lord, quicken my wits," and I knew in an instant what was next.

"What did the baby eat?" I asked. They started to tell how she had eaten what they had. The mother was taking very long to get there, but I knew what I had to do.

I took the child into my room, put my finger down the throat, and turned her over quickly. Up it all came. I cleaned her up and saw that the problem had been solved, so I sat with her in the rocking chair waiting for the mother.

By the time the mother arrived, she must have wondered what the excitement was all about, but when I took her in the room and she saw what had come out of the baby her only comment was,

"Of my God! Thanks, Teacher," and they all went away happy, yet not realizing the seriousness of the event.

Twins

This tea cup business caught up with me there and people began to want their fortunes told. I tried to say no, but one quiet evening Violet, who had recently got married, came to see me requesting that I tell her fortune. She had really come to ask me to make her a

Chapter Three: Turks and Caicos Islands

layette, but she brought her cup along in a paper bag. I argued against it, but with her pleading, I gave in.

Before I knew it, I said, "Twins!" Violet really got thrown off for she had been to the doctor earlier and he said no such thing. I tried to cover it up, but that girl went straight to the doctor saying I told her she would have twins! He was at my house in no time for everyone was close to everyone else. He was very put out with me.

"Why did you tell this girl a thing like that? I am the doctor here and you have really upset her. The bad thing is that she believes what you say." He stormed out, and I knew I was in trouble with someone who was really my friend.

Violet came back and I told her I should not have said what I did because I was not the doctor. My heart still said twins, but I had to deny that for her sake.

She came to me many times. I made up the layette for her and she really seemed to have forgotten about twins. When I learned that her mother had more than one set of twins, I was even more certain that my heart was correct. But what could I do?

She asked me to promise that when she was ready to have the baby I would be there. Things seemed to go very well and then the day came. Early one Saturday, one of her brothers came with a message—his sister wanted me to come right away. So, as I promised, I went.

Violet was in labor and both the doctor and the midwife were there. There was trouble for the baby seemed to be blocked. Time went by and the doctor realized he would have to take the baby. They had a very large dining room table, so we put sheets on and ironed them. Her brothers and her husband lifted her from the bed to the table.

Such bleeding there was, but she was conscious.

"Ms. V, please pray for me," she pleaded.

By this time her mother, aunts and other relatives had moved out of the house and were all sitting in the yard weeping.

I stood near her head and cooled it with Bay Rum. She seemed to be aware. Then the doctor wanted some light as he would have to take the baby with forceps. Someone brought a good flashlight and he asked me to hold it so he could see what he was doing with the help of the nurse. I tried to hold it steady, but that was hard to do. The doctor worked and brought the infant out, a little girl—dead. He breathed hard.

Suddenly the nurse called out, "doctor, doctor, there's another baby!"

In a few minutes the baby was out, another little girl, this one alive, but not well. There was just too much blood leaving my friend's body and as we were in this place, there was no chance of a transfusion. I thought of her strong husband and all her big healthy brothers who would have given their blood, if there were a way for her to get it.

"Put her on the bed," the doctor ordered and that was done. Her pastor was there and he prayed for her, then went out. There was such sadness in that yard. Everyone had given up.

I stayed with great difficulty, but knew it would not be long for her. She was still conscious, in and out, but she said again,

"Ms. V, pray for me."

I bent close to her and said the Twenty-third Psalm and the Lord's Prayer, and begged God to help us.

"Any Enos?" she asked. I realized that the blood loss was creating thirst.

"My God," I said, "When your son lost his blood, he thirsted. This girl is saying, 'I thirst, too.' Please help us."

I relayed the need and all the young ones went through the little town in no time. No Enos was to be had anywhere! No Enos fruit salts. Her dying felt need could not be satisfied. I felt terrible and could only offer my tears.

"My Mama," she said, and I called for her mother, who was agonizing for her one girl among eleven boys. She did not want to see her child dying, but I was able to get her to come.

"Kiss her," I said, "Kiss her while she can feel you for she called for you." she put her arms around this lovely child of hers, kissed her and had to be taken away.

The pain of grief is felt in the midbody area. There is nothing like it and those who have lost loved ones really know of what I speak. The head aches, the heart aches, everywhere is involved, but what goes on in that solar plexus area is a thing in itself. It is the wrenching away place. Perhaps it is there for the connecting point. The navel connecting mother to child and on and on for generations is broken and our deepest feelings die hard.

She still breathed, but she was slowly going from us. I held her hands, I whispered in her ear, "God loves you, God is your shepherd, you are in His care, Jesus loves you, you are his."

Oh, the weeping was everywhere and then very peacefully, I thought how these twins had come and one would go with her. The other was so weak, she may go, too. Quietly, beautifully, her life ebbed away and then it was all over. She was beautiful in life and even in death her inexpressible beauty was there. What grief there was, too, for this was such a beloved young person and death seemed to be a real enemy. We tied up her jaw, tied her feet together, covered her and left her alone for awhile.

I went home with many questions. I thought of the doctor and then someone noticed that he was not around. I realized I had to find him. I knew he would feel very sad because of what had happened. He had to be somewhere on the rocks, hidden by the bushes and looking at the sea. He used to do that often as he read.

He was a broken man. "Why didn't I listen to you?" he said.

"You had no reason to, because I could never prove to you, not even to myself, where I got it. If you act like this, you will never be able to work here. You had no x-ray, no tools to help you. You know that many times when twins are up and down, it is difficult to pick up that back heartbeat."

The first baby, the one he took away, was big and strong. The other was small and weak. It is my opinion that the small one somehow moved down longing for life just as much as the first, and was in the way.

"Learn from your mistake. The only thing you might have done was to send her to Grand Turk if you had any questions, but then you had none, so you did the best you knew how to do."

He walked to our house where the mother of our three little girls took him aside for advice. She saw to it that he had some food, for he lived alone and would probably have gone without food.

I was weary and sad beyond expression, but I was satisfied that I had kept my promise to be with her on that day.

But, of the questions that came as I tried to rest, to keep it all outside of me where I could see it, look at it and hopefully find some answers. What should I have done with my sense of twins? Maybe I could have talked the doctor into sending her the twenty-two sea miles for an x-ray. I expected her to have twins, but I truly believed that as healthy as she was right up to the point of labour, everything was going to be fine. I was so wrong!

A Vision and a Dream

Early one morning I was half awake when I saw a coffin with a man in it right in my doorway. I knew

CHAPTER THREE: Turks and Caicos Islands

the man, so I woke up the rest of the household and told what I had seen. The mother of the family jumped up, put on her clothes quickly, and went to his house to tell him not to go fishing, but he had already left. Usually, he returned by eleven but not today, so they went looking for him.

He was found dead in his boat and we all felt sad. He was a lively old man with a large family. A grandson was on the school staff and a number of grandchildren were in school. In this kind of place, work was over for the day.

My questions were, "how could that be seen at around six o'clock in the morning? When did he really die? Was the information to be given so the search for him could take place then, not five hours later?" There were no answers at all.

I had a dream of seeing a field of tall green leaves and, as I looked, an angel wafted down, picked three leaves and took them up and out of sight. It was its own message of an event to be, but to whom? I told several people but nobody knew any more than I did.

At ten o'clock, we heard a dreadful waling from where men were working on the salt mounds. Someone stopped by to tell us that a piece of the salt mound had broken off and flattened three workers.

"Now, God," I thought, "why couldn't you have told me which three men and let me warn them of danger? What was the purpose behind a dream like that? Just to see it come pass?" I got no answers.

A Trip to North Caicos

Two of us took a trip to North Caicos to talk about starting a YWCA club. The outward journey was wonderful. The breezes were just right; the beauty all around was indescribable and soon we arrived at what was known as Bottle Creek, so-named because one sailed through a long creek and then into a beautiful bay.

We were met by a group of ladies who took us up to the school where we freshened up and talked about the YWCA and starting a club. I was introduced to sassafras tea, which I did not like very well, but it was their drink and it was supposed to be a wonderful tonic.

After the meeting, we went to the home of a very dear lady whose presence was very powerful indeed. I sensed a great depth of love here and, as I sat on her porch looking at the beauty of the bay, I had such a sense of peace, of worship, of unity with all things.

We had a good meal and then went for a walk. People were very friendly, and as we returned home, I found that I was really ready for bed. People in those parts stuffed their mattresses with dried grass and the smell of the grass as I lay to rest made me feel that she had the mattress freshly fixed up for us. I have never slept on a mattress like this before. It was not uncomfortable, but it was strange. I took a long time to fall asleep, but I did and never woke until the sun's rays moved in to say, "Hello". I got up, tidied up, and went outside. It was beautiful and I thought of a hymn that said,

> Come, O Lord, like morning sunlight,
> Making all life new and free;
> For the daily task and challenge
> May we rise renewed in thee.
> Come, O Lord, like ocean flood-tides,
> Flowing inland from the sea;
> As the waters fill the shallows,
> May our souls be filled with Thee.

(Milton S. Littlefield, *Hymns for Creative Living*, Judson Press, Chicago)

To be out there with nature at her best, to breathe in this air that seemed to want me to be as light and as invisible as itself, gave me the feeling that I was part of everything around me—sun, sea, sky, air, grass, fish. Oh, everything felt like glory.

CHAPTER THREE: Turks and Caicos Islands

My childhood days in the gallery of St. John's Cathedral singing what is known as the Benedicite, broke into mind. "Praise Him and Magnify Him Forever!" I sat on a log by the bay and sang it. I felt the praise throughout my being. Then I walked up the slope to the house. I was ready for breakfast.

My friend and I planned to return the next day. In the early evening, we were seeing what they called the Northern Lights. What a beautiful sky!

At seven o'clock that night the captain of the little boat came to say we should get ready to leave by eight. The lights meant that we would have a storm in twenty-four hours. If we left then, we would be in East Harbour long before noon.

We agreed and with a few johnny cakes, some water, a thermos of tea and a cargo of grass, we left. We had to sail through the long creek to get to the sea and going through we fell asleep. The captain's son was left to steer us through and he was to wake his father when he cleared the creek.

By the time his father woke up, we were far away from land in low tide and lost. We sailed through the channel, hit bottom, turned around and sailed only to hit bottom all day. As the sun went down, we were just as far from anywhere as we were when the old man woke up. There were no stars to guide him and he knew, just as we did, that the storm he was trying to avoid would find us hopelessly lost at sea, and in danger of being blown to deep water from which we could not return.

All of us were tired. The old man spoke. "Try to see if you see any mangrove in the sea." All day long when we were in very shallow water, there were little clumps of mangrove, but this was night and a stormy night.

I promised God everything I could if He would bring us safely through the storm. Oh, what great things I would do for Him. I prayed for forgiveness of all my sins. That wind was terrific. Then with so much lightning, the son thought he saw a dark spot. The boat was in shallow water and we all tried to use our poles to get the boat there. When we got close to a small clump of mangrove, the captain said he would throw the anchor into the bushes to see if it would lock onto the roots.

After several tries, the anchor held, but the rope was thin and we wondered if it would hold. An awesome feeling was present, for the boat was full of water and we were too tired to bail it out. The boat was not leaking, but the rain poured in torrents and the rough sea put its quota in. We just sat in it, hauled the sail over us, and all four of us went to sleep! Yes, we all went to sleep.

Gradually the storm blew over and slowly, as we woke, we bailed the boat. We saw signs of the day breaking, so we knew which was east for sure.

The sail was of no use as something on the mast head was broken. The son tried to climb the mast to fix what was wrong. He was able to tie in the rope to hold the sail but the sail fell down. He managed to tie on the jib and the old man pulled on the anchor rope. He had a bit of trouble extracting it from the roots, but as the water was shallow, the son went overboard and got it out. So, we set sail.

It was not long before we saw sails coming in from several directions. "They are out looking for us," the old man said. "They know we left Bottle Creek and had not reached East harbor so we had to be out in the storm."

What joy the searchers had as they came near us! Someone was able to fix the sail so we stayed in our own boat. It was past two in the afternoon when we dropped anchor. They carried us ashore and all those who had come to see us clapped for joy. They told us how they have prayed for us through the night. We walked home tired to the bone, but thankful.

I did not want any food, only rest. I got a warm bath, drank some Ovaltine and went to sleep. When I awoke, the whole episode was like a nightmare instead of a reality. It took me a few days to recover fully, but I found new meaning in the words of the well-known hymn, "Will your anchor hold in the storms of life?" It is true that unless we are grounded deep in the Saviour's love, we cannot weather the storm.

Being Put Out of the Anglican Church

As an Anglican I was soon asked to help with church tasks and became a Vestry member, an officer of the church. Because the Anglican priests live in Grand Turk, the capital, they generally came every six weeks, but often the period stretched to two months. The Lay Reader acted for the priest and people went to church whether it was Lay Reader or Priest.

The Vestry members were assigned topics to prepare the candidates for Confirmation. I was asked to take two topics, Transubstantiation and Confession. Transubstantiation refers to the belief that the communion wine becomes the blood of Jesus Christ and the bread becomes His body. It is no longer a symbol, but the substance actually changes. Confession means that the priest acts as an intermediary between the person and God. I just said I was sorry, that I could not teach something in which I did not believe.

We had neither of those in the Anglican Church in British Honduras. We were part of the church in Jamaica, which was low church. But the church in Turks and Caicos was part of the Anglican Church in the Bahamas, which was high church. So, at South Caicos they were high church; they believed in both transubstantiation and confession.

The lay minister turned red, and he was so angry that he could hardly finish the meeting.

"If you do not believe in these essential doctrines of the faith, then you are a heretic to the faith," he shouted.

I explained my stand on confession, that it is essential, but not through a priest. I stood up, and all the members of the committee stood up, too, but I discouraged them from leaving.

I said, "No, no, this is your faith. You have grown up believing this way, but I don't believe this way and I'm not going to teach it. So, I can't be on the church committee."

And then I turned to him and made my classic statement, "Since this church belongs to you, you can put me out. But I belong to the church for which Christ died and you can't put me out of that." And I went.

I was barred from all activities to do with the church. I was hurt, but maybe that event set the course for my future journey among Friends.

Later the Archdeacon said, "The man had no right, only the Bishop can excommunicate somebody like that. We would have an inquiry. He can't put you out like that."

The Bishop, when he came for Confirmation, said, "Oh no, no, please return"

But he did put me out and I accepted the put out, anyway. I had no idea that the Anglican Church resorted to such tactics. But, as secure as I was in the faith, rather than in the denomination, I could worship with the Methodists and the Baptists and later found the Ecumenical Movement to be a very important fact of life.

To base faith on doctrine is useless, but to build a fellowship of believers who are assured of salvation in Christ, even where there is not understanding and maybe outright disagreement with doctrine, the claim to salvation by the blood of Jesus Christ is a basis for unity. The rest will have to go as we find God's spirit at work removing the unessentials. The period of enlightenment is already here. It may take twenty years, maybe fifty, but it must come if Christianity is to survive. The Universal Church, the Church Victorious, is a surety, so all who think the future of the church rests with doctrine will someday learn the truth.

When I went back to Jamaica I did not feel like going back into the Anglican Church even though it was low church. I had broken with it. I did not know where I was going.

Leaving Turks and Caicos

I thank the Lord for all the little nooks and corners He put me in. I had to see what I would make of them. After five years of life in this place, where so many important learnings took place, I knew the time had come to set sail for the continuing journey. I was ready in spite of the uncertainty for what was next. That internal mechanism, the urge that says, "It's time to move on," knows that already the next phase of the journey had started.

CHAPTER FOUR
Highgate (1950-56)

This school was a sort of discovery place, for all those who had taken the exam before were not dullards. They were generally very good students who had one or two weaknesses. At Conti, teachers set out to discover those basic weaknesses and to use every means at their disposal to correct the weaknesses and send the students on their way to success.

When I came back from South Caicos, Ruby Meredith knew I was back and said,

"I know you just came back and you want to rest, but there is a job in Highgate and I believe you could help those children. A lot of them failed their exams. But you will have to go on Monday."

That meant I had just two days. In the meantime another friend said,

"I am waiting on you. I heard you are coming. I have a place for you. I want to start a secondary school and I want you and me to do it Kingston."

The Condensory, where condensed milk was made, was starting a school for the children of their employees. They wanted me to teach in their primary school, but I was not interested in that. I thought about helping my friend with that secondary school, but Ruby Meredith came with such an appeal. And she told me what it was all about that I would go to Highgate and there would be

CHAPTER FOUR: Highgate

a place for me to live. And that is how I went to Highgate. And that is how the fact that she was a Quaker came into play because it was a Friends School. I did not know who Friends were then.

Yes, this is Highgate, the same Highgate where, in 1942, the bus broke down and I was helped by Dan and Val, where I slept next to the wall. I had news of Dan's death. The story was that he died of tetanus and Val had given up Highgate and was living in Kingston where she worked for a doctor. I tried to find her without success.

Highgate, as its name implies, is high and is like a gate to many other places. At the top of the hill on which the centre of town sits, there are roads that seem to lead to everywhere. The view from this point is magnificent.

My sojourn here would begin a little way from town at a cottage known as Windyridge, for it stood on the eastern side of a hill and received the fresh breezes from the sea. Below the cottage lay a valley. Highgate will ever be fresh in my memory, for there many very important learnings occurred.

Continuation School

The school known as the Continuation School, called "Conti" by everybody, was truly one of a kind. The idea behind it could only have come from the Religious Society of Friends. Friends had been working in India and heard about Indians going to Jamaica as indentured servants. Friends came to Jamaica to work with these indentured servants. The Continuation School was part of that work.

The atmosphere of Conti was one of encouraging success. No one was written off. A boy had been given a note to take home concerning a meeting, but no one showed up from the staff of the Boy's Home where he lived. When it was time for the next meeting, the principal gave the same boy the notice for the staff. One of the teachers reminded her of the boy's previous failure. She said she had to help him to be a success and she was not about to remind him of the past failure. She was sure he would not fail this time and she was right, he did not.

There were only three of us for the ninety students but what a team! What students! All were into getting an education. For some, it was the last time they would be allowed to sit the famous Third Year Examination set by the Education Department.

This school was a sort of discovery place, for all those who had taken the exam before were not dullards. They were generally very good students who had one or two weaknesses. At Conti, teachers set out to discover those basic weaknesses and to use every means at their disposal to correct the weaknesses and send the students on their way to success.

For most of the students, regular class work was enough. They were required to do maximum work even as teachers gave maximum delivery. Some had such basic weaknesses that it took everything in the making of a real teacher to find special ways of moving to the level of that weakness and slowly, patiently, in faith, rebuild new structures.

There was the lad who did not know when to use "is" or "his". The use or non-use of the aspirate, "h" was the problem. How does a teacher help a seventeen-year-old to learn that? There was a girl of eighteen who never seemed to have heard of finite verbs. Words ending in "ing" were predominant and sentences would be half a page long! How could that problem be licked? In these two cases, each student was as smart as they come in learning facts.

In the case of the girl, she was a sort of mathematical wizard. She could do ten sums in half the time it took everyone else in the class to do them and every one was correct! I asked her how she learned her mathematics. To my astonishment, she said she just knew. Had someone picked up the weakness in English, this student might have gone on to be an Open Scholar.

CHAPTER FOUR: *Highgate*

The third student who challenged me was a boy who became asthmatic whenever he heard the word "test". He had to be cared for, but he was a very smart youngster and generally outstanding.

The fourth was a student who with all his smartness was over-meticulous. Everything had to be just so and he spent a lot of time starting over. With him there were no mistakes but he was never able to finish enough work to get a pass. How could he be helped?

The fifth, another smart lad, had an illegible handwriting. Sure, he could tell everything he had written, but no one else could read what he wrote. It was impossible! It was not cover-up. He knew his facts, but, now that I write of it, some of his papers should have been kept for scientific study.

Maybe you would like to hear how God helped me to help these wonderful young hopefuls. First, the lad with the "is-his", "and-hand", etc. He must have written pages and pages of fill-in activity sheets. "John is." "The baby is." "This paper is." I drilled him with using Is correctly. Then I did the same with "his"—"his hat", "his book", "his work", "his hand". Then I moved to "this is his hat." And "that is his book", leaving the two dashes for him to fill in. "This __ __ mother." "__ mother __ here." Quietly we worked together. Some words he just had to learn to spell, like "heavy". It took him a long time to work on "and" and "hand", but eventually he could pronounce and use each correctly.

He was a big handsome lad who wanted to be a policeman. He towered over me, but was soft spoken and well mannered. He was able to make it and went on to the career of his choice.

Now for the girl who was really a genius. She was full of ideas, and yet for her, the participle was the thing. Even when she read aloud what she had written, she could not feel the wrongness of the structures. She wrote long paragraphs with nary a finite verb. She also had no use for past tense. It was always "I was going" and sometimes "I were going" and "they was going", faults that should have been corrected long ago. Her spelling was near perfect.

It took us a long time to start getting anywhere. I went to my room with her work in hand. I knelt down and told God that he had sent her there because she needed us. I said, "Look at this work. What am I to do about it?" I made the point that this was her last chance and I needed wisdom.

The next day I decided to do a similar thing as I was doing with the first lad, but this would take more out of me. This girl had a two-mile walk to and from school, so I could not keep her as long as I wanted to. I agreed to keep her twice weekly after school and then use odd moments of the day to do extras.

I worked on the use of the past tense. We wrote up hundreds of words and repeated them together. Somehow, I felt that doing it together was valuable. We did singular and then went on to plurals. Then I tried letting her correct me. I said things like "John were going" and after awhile she got it very well. It was a lot of work, but she finally came to it.

We did not have too much time, but I had one strategy left. Short sentences. Why not? Together we wrote out ten compositions that she had to study. We also wrote ten typical letters.

With true or false this girl would have shocked examiners with correct answers. With essay questions she was hopeless. I told her to put down "1" and write the first fact. I showed her how to combine two facts with use of conjunctions and relative pronouns. She worked hard at it and because she knew facts, her attention was on dealing with her special problems.

She answered all sorts of questions and after awhile she mastered answering questions by numbering her points. After all, it would be very clear to an examiner that she really knew her facts and that was what she

CHAPTER FOUR: Highgate

was giving him/her. I prayed for her to get a letter to write rather than an essay on the examination.

Time came for forms to be sent in and she was not accepted to be on the school's list. True, her problems were not all over, but great improvement had been made. I was really annoyed about it, so I decided to sign her in as a private candidate.

I told the girl I was sending her as a private candidate and she did not care. All she wanted was to be entered. We continued to work and she continued to improve. All of a sudden, I realized that it was like teaching her something for the first time and she was now ready to learn this as something new. This was the key and I knew she would do very well in the exam. I did not share what I was doing with anyone.

Long afterwards I understood why that was good. I was listening to a sermon that taught me something akin to the Creole proverb, "No everything good fu noh, good to tak." This preacher was speaking about Herod and the Wise Men and what they had found out about the young child. In their wisdom, they heeded the warning they received in a dream and went home by another way. Oh, yes, how often have not the Herods of the world killed off somebody's young child in the form of new ideas. That sermon really showed me an important fact I have never forgotten.

So exam day came. I was sure my girl would make it. This was her last chance, remember. She had to make it.

The teachers were waiting at the school when she came. She was so excited! She knelt down by my chair and put her arms around me. She started to cry. I began to wonder if anything had gone wrong. I got up and went with her to one of the staff rooms. She showed me her arithmetic paper and I believed she had 100%. Then she said, "I made it. I know I made it. I got a letter to write and I know I did it right." As I looked at that paper, my own eye filled with tears, for I knew she had made it.

I had other students to hear from and went out to hear from them. They too felt good about their work. Except for two girls I would not have entered because they were not ready, I believed all the others would make it.

We all had to wait for the famous *Gazette* with the list of successful candidates. When the names did come out the teachers looked under Highgate Continuation School, but I had to look at what was number one for me—Private Candidates. Oh yes, there her name was and five credits. My girl was on her way. She passed the test to go to England for nurses training. She was successful and the last news I had of her was that she had sent for her parents. Even though I could not see that meeting, I was happy to hear of her continued success and I was sure she would give excellent nursing care wherever she went.

The asthmatic lad was quite another thing. I had never dealt with this kind of problem before, but there had to be a way to help him. He was such a good student, but where did that put him if he could not sit for exams? He was too smart to write off. He wanted to be a teacher and he had the makings of getting to the top, but this asthma was a real knockout thing.

In God's dealings with Israel, there is some place where it says something like this, "How can I give thee up, Oh Ephrain?"

My heart ached for this lad and I made up my mind to try a head-on attack. Usually I let him out of class when his wheezing started, but I decided to risk a "no", but give him extra care. It was a kind of plot, but I had to try it. I told the class what I had planned because they would get upset and maybe be thrown off and get low marks in the test.

I went to school armed with Bay Rum, smelling salts, two big handkerchiefs and courage. The test was written up and in a few minutes he was ready for tests as usual, so I sat by him and told him I only wanted him to do enough to pass.

CHAPTER FOUR: Highgate

He was wheezing, he had a headache, and his tears were too copious for comfort. I wet his head with Bay Rum; I gave him a careful whiff of smelling salts; and I wiped the sweat from his face while I urged him to try to write. It was a very easy mathematics test and I sat by him on the edge of the class nearest to what was called the side room. We could make a quick exit if necessary. He did three and then I had to give up, but it was 30% better than zero. I let him out of class praising him for what he had done. Next test would undoubtedly be easier.

It got better and better and he did not need the same pressure for all his subjects. If we could ride it out with mathematics, he would get a pass and go on up to the A which he could easily make. In time he made his pass and then I think he realized that pass was not good enough. He was good at mathematics and should get an A. He also realized what this would do to his total grades and his place in the class.

Yes, I did not have to say a thing to him. The struggle was over and he, too, was on his way. In later years, he became Principal of the School!

Some of the students at the time really thought I was hard. They did not believe it would work at all, because the lad had asthma, and as far as they knew he would continue to have it. But when success came, they said I was right to try.

The lad himself said he felt that I was cruel because I knew he had asthma, but now that he looked back, he realized that it was right for I was seeing then what he could only see in retrospect.

The meticulous lad was the youngest in the class, so he had more time than the others did. It would take a one-to-one plan to help him overcome his problems and I had to make the difficult decision to let him wait a year.

He read well, was an excellent speller, and knew his mathematics concepts, but his written output was hopeless. He was handsome and took care of his belongings. He was never rude and he played games quite well, but there were to be no errors corrected on his papers. His exercise books were thin because he tore out the pages that had any corrections. If he wrote a word wrongly and had to correct, there was no way to do it except to start over.

The lad was in need of some psychological counselling. Clothes, shoes, hair, everything about him showed his internal situation. He would need some pressure too, because he was a perfectionist of a strange order. He was without known family. He was always deadly serious, not laughing at jokes and indeed showing that part of him was tied up and securely stored somewhere.

He was very smart, but painstakingly slow so that he never got beyond 40 percent. The fact he did not get passing grades did not seem to bother him. He wanted to be an Accountant. He struck me as being a very old man even though he was only fourteen. He fascinated me. One day I sat beside him as he worked, for I had to try to help him with the starting over business. He cried and then gave up. I barred him from using pens. I thought that using pencils he could erase the errors. That did not work either. He was good at orals. Unfortunately for me, I had to work with another class and he had a new teacher who became very frustrated with his output. I never knew what happened to him.

A Concert at Highgate

I invited my friend, Helen Craig, to come to Jamaica from British Honduras for a visit. Helen was a child prodigy musician. At eight years old she was given a scholarship to study music abroad, but her father had just died and she was not able to accept that scholarship. Eventually she did go to New York for a long career as a pianist. While Helen was visiting me at Highgate, she and Lola Cadogan gave a concert.

CHAPTER FOUR: *Highgate*

Lola Cadogan was the wife of Methodist minister Claude Cadogan, a Belizean who was saved in our house in the 1931 hurricane. They were living in Kingston at the time. He could really preach and she sang beautifully. I invited some people from Kingston to Highgate for the concert and they all came. We moved the tables out of the dining room and had a wonderful time. People talked about it for years afterward. Highgate had never seen such a thing!

A Call for Help

It was a wild, stormy day in Highgate, and the rain poured in torrents. There could be no school, no business, nothing outside could go on. These days were few but they became very important days for me.

I am a short-wave radio fan and I was listening to "Back to the bible". Theodore Epp was preaching, but suddenly, as if it were over the waves, I heard a call. It was a call for help from someone whose voice I knew immediately. It was a prayer to God to send help and I heard it again. I was troubled for the weather was somewhat worse and I knew it would be difficult to get to her house.

I went to the matron and told what had taken place.

"I must find a way to go," I told her, "I have to go."

She understood the urgency, but we could not decide what to do. I thought of a taxi-man who had a telephone, but the phone was dead.

After a few minutes the matron said she did not see how I could go, how the taxi-man could not get to me. I kept trying to dial and finally got him, and he said he would try to get there.

It was a rough trip as the rain kept pouring, but he made it and we were able to get to the house. The door was unlocked and I went in, but I asked the taxi-man to wait until I sized up the situation.

My friend said, "Thank God!'

She explained that she was losing a lot of blood and was unable to get to the telephone, so she prayed and asked God to send someone to help her. I realized that she needed medical help, so I asked the taxi driver to go for the doctor who was about a half mile away. I sent a note so he could understand the urgency and would know what medicines to bring. It was good that his office was at his house.

He came and said it was serious as she had lost a lot of blood. He gave her an injection and left other medicine and instructions that required someone to be with her. As I was not busy, I was able to stay through the night. By the next day she was all right to be alone.

Does the human being have what is similar to an antenna that is able to receive calls such as these? This was a deeply spiritual person and her call was received by another spiritually aware person.

Thousands of people have had similar experiences. Are we missing out on a significant area of service, the "SOS" and "May Day" calls for help that are sent out all the time? Are there other ways of responding? Would my response have been useful if I had simply offered a prayer?

A Terrifying Dream

One morning I woke up after a terrifying dream. I was nervous and afraid to leave the house, though I knew I had to go to school. I was not ill and my class would be waiting. The dream went like this:

I was on my way to school when just at the railway junction, I saw a girl on a bicycle and a little dog beside her. Coming from the right was the doctor in his car. He did not, really could not, see the girl coming up the grade. Coming around the left curve was a truck. I could not see it but heard it grinding its way around the slope. As the girl got on the bike with the dog running beside her, she turned almost in the doctor's path and he swerved to avoid her and the dog, just as the truck came around the bend. The car bounced against the truck and was

CHAPTER FOUR: Highgate

turned in the opposite direction. As the truck driver put on his brakes, some men in the back of the truck were flung up and over and some just lay on the ground as though they were dead or injured. I was standing about six inches from the front wheel of the truck with my back against a barbed wire fence.

So, I really wanted someone to go along with me. The Senior Matron was very busy; the yard boy was out; and nobody could understand my fear of the road. I finally got the children's matron to agree to go and we set out.

We were no sooner in the very spot where I was in the dream when the whole thing went off as I had seen it in my dream. The only difference was that in the dream I was alone, but in the event someone was with me.

If I lie on my back, I go into another world. I see lots colours, all colours of the rainbow swirling around. That is the way the visions start, but if I turn over, I can stop it. So, I pile up pillows beside me in bed so I never roll over onto my back. I do not want to see the visions because they relate to the future and I am prepared to live one day at a time. If it is going to happen anyway, if I cannot change anything, I do not want to know.

Friends Meeting

That first Sunday after I went to teach in Highgate, I went to Friends Meeting. Somewhere in the ten minutes of silence I realized that I had the freedom to think what I liked about Jesus Christ. It was the first knowing that came to me, that I could think anything, that I did not have to tell my mind that it is sinful to think this or to ask that. I grew up where it was felt that your beliefs were set and you did not go outside of them. Year in and year out, it becomes a part of you. So, that was a great thing that happened to me that Sunday. I felt a freedom to ask questions of myself, not of anybody else in there, but of myself, to ask questions about Jesus Christ. I could think what I like and allow my mind to think or not think. I had a freedom about the scriptures. I did not have to believe what anyone else told me at all. At the time I was nowhere. I had just come from South Caicos where I was put out of the Anglican Church because I did not believe in transubstantiation and confession to the priest. So that is how I became involved with Friends.

It took me a year to decide that this was really what I wanted. I read. I read a lot. I was friendly with everybody. I went to meeting every Sunday. We had to go with the students. I did not find anything to disagree with in the *Faith and Practice*. So I said,

"I could live with that."

And I just liked the ways of Friends. I liked the form of worship, the quiet, and I could ask all the questions I wanted. I still have that kind of mind now, still a lot of questions. When they were taking about membership for the next year, whether anybody was interested in being a member, I said I would like to be a member.

I had to take some classes learning all about Friends. That is how I became a Friend. I became a member of Highgate Friends Church. I was teaching at the school at the same time. The school did not have any specifically Friends religious training. The schoolbooks were set for the year by the government. One year might be on the gospel of Mark and you had to deal with that because all the questions on the exam would be on the gospel of Mark. But it did not have anything to do with Friends except the Sunday School. You got teaching in the Sunday School. The school had worship every morning, a hymn and a Bible reading every day.

Lyndale

While I was teaching at Continuation, Margaret Davis was the Principal at Lyndale, the Girl's Home at Highgate, and she had asked me to come for the vacation. She went to the States and married Merle Davis, so she did not return. I was there, so they asked

CHAPTER FOUR: *Highgate* 107

me, "Would you carry on until we can know what we are going to do?"

It was a good thing it was summertime and Lyndale had people that knew what they were doing. After that I still taught at the Continuation School, but I also managed Lyndale. They appointed me Principal and I was there for five and a half years.

In 1957 it came time for me to move on. I was convinced I had done all I could there and had learned what I had been called there to learn. I was ready for a new or different kind of experience.

I did not want to return to British Honduras at that time because it could not provide me with the new experiences that I desired. To my way of thinking, religion had captivated us in British Honduras and we were not ready to ask the questions that troubled us. So, I took advantage of the opportunity offered to me to go to the United States.

Friends Conference in Greensboro

I used to write to the people who sponsored girls at Lyndale and Evelyn Kendall somehow liked what I said in my letters. We got to be pen pals. She wrote, "Whenever you want to come to the States, we will sponsor you."

Her husband was a big-time businessman, so there were no money problems. I made application for a green card and got it quickly.

There was to be a Friends conference in the United States that I wanted to attend. By the time I applied, others had been selected and I accepted that. However, early one morning as I meditated, I was aware of a spiritual presence at the head of my bed. I did not question it, but remained in thought.

"You are to get things ready to go to the Conference. Get ready, for you will go." That was all—then the presence faded away.

At the breakfast table I mentioned the experience to the others, who called it wishful thinking. I went to church and found things were set. Those to go were all going. Next week was the same thing. Anyway, I had a green card, so did not need a visa, but I had to get my clothing prepared and needed to visit the hairdresser. I did these things on Monday and Tuesday. On Wednesday I had a phone call from the Clerk of the Meeting. Eula Mae had dropped out, others had been checked but no one else had a visa so there was no one who could be ready to leave on Friday. They asked if I could do it. I told them, "Yes, I can go." It was just as I had been told.

So, in 1954 I went to the United States for the first time. When I got to the Friends Conference in Greensboro, North Carolina, they were short of one leader, so they asked me to lead a study group. That is how I met Clifford and Anna Lydia Hadley. They were sold on my presentation.

That paved the way for me to move to the United States three years later. As they promised, the Kendalls sponsored my application for a Resident Visa in the USA. It took quite some time to get all the correct papers in order, but they were very persistent until finally I gained permission to reside in the United States.

CHAPTER FIVE
Sojourns in the United States (1957-2008)

I have spoken in many places in the U.S. and they have given me the freedom to say some big things to them. They really listened to me. They accepted my terms and more of them left with something they had not heard before, but it answered questions they had in their minds. I know that I made an impact there. A lot of people taped my speeches. I think that I was saying some old things in a new way. I recently got a letter from someone talking about what I said in a speech in Greensboro. That was a long time ago and she still remembers.

Practical Nurse Training

In 1957 I went to the USA and stayed with my Aunt Agnes in Indianapolis. I was not allowed to teach because I did not have the proper credentials for the USA and I did not want to do domestic work. My aunt had told me about the nurses training at the Indiana University Medical Center. I applied and was accepted. In those days the tuition was paid for by the State. I never liked to go out in the winter, so I took a room in the Medical Center.

There was a big difference between the white and coloured students. I played between the two because I was neither. The students regarded me as different from the American coloured. I was a point of reference for both sides. I was fully accepted by the whites and the blacks.

I never had any problem, but between them there were problems. This was a highly rated school of nursing, second only to one in New York. It was very strict. The coloured girls tried to get over without putting on a clean uniform every day. They had to work so hard just to make ends meet to go to school and keep their families. When they came to school, they would be sleepy because they had worked all night. They never had time to wash their uniforms. The school would pull them out of class and embarrass them. The white students never had to do any of that. America is very good in some ways, but uncaring in others. If the students had to work two shifts, it was no one else's business. Maybe the school did not realize they had to work like that. I could never have done it.

I cannot say the white students ever really showed any prejudice, but because the blacks know about prejudice and they feel it, they expect it. I consider myself on the shy side, but when I am making moves, I have to talk to myself. None of those white students were better than me. Why should I put myself down for them? Although I could not teach in the USA, my teaching experience gave me an ability to express myself, which helped in nursing.

There was a nice young white girl who was hanging out with the white crowd, drinking, smoking, and staying out late. One day she came to my room. She was crying and said,

"I want to ask you a big favour. If my mother knew what kind of life I am living, she would die. She's a good Christian woman. And I'm out drinking and smoking and carrying on. Would you let me stay here with you?"

It was the best thing I ever did. The girl cleaned my shoes every day and washed my uniform. She looked after me. She said,

"When my mother comes, you tell her how good I have been to you. Don't tell her how I started out bad."

CHAPTER FIVE: Sojourns in the United States

She was white. I was coloured, and we lived together well. She asked me about prayer and God because she had never gone to church.

The fact that I was not American was often a saving grace. When she was having her engagement dinner, she had quite a problem to find a place that would accept me. Finally, she called one place, said I was from Central America and they agreed to having me there.

They elected me the Chaplain of the class. Once a week we had worship and I arranged that. When the students had problems, they came to me and I helped them work it out.

When graduation time came, I had made equal points on the tests as a white girl, but I had come in two days late, so on the attendance I could not get 100. They gave her the highest award and the American black students protested, saying it was favoritism. They made a big thing of it and the whole school was divided. As Chaplain, I had to counsel them. I told them the school was right to give her the award and they must not protest.

After the one-year training program, I did another year of specialized training with premature infants, on the medical ward, and on the psychiatric ward.

Preemies

Training with premature infants was terrible, mainly because of my heightened sensitivity to the infants. They were very interesting beings as they longed for life. They stirred, blinked and gave signs that it was time to be fed. They were so very fragile and one wished to find how to give them that one thing that would make them spark off so they could go to their mothers who waited with such desire for their babies to be in their arms.

As a girl, I had seen a preemie cared for in a shoebox to begin with. It was cozy for she did not have all that space like there was in the incubator. There were three sides, places to touch that were soft and somehow warm enough. A doctor came in with a baby, a preemie. He was a new doctor and had not experienced this before. He was shaking. He was so nervous that he forgot to bring the chart, so he had to go back for it before I could admit the baby officially.

They had all given up on the baby for dead because she was not likely to live, but I thought she should have proper care regardless.

Later the nurse came on her rounds and checked to see if I had admitted the baby correctly. She asked me if I had baptized the baby. When I said no, the nurse baptized the infant and charted the event. But she was so careless about it all.

Every chance I had I went by and talked lovingly to the child and found her situation stabilizing. We went through the night and just before the change of duty, the nurse that had baptized the child really believed that the child could not have lasted the night. I reported and left, praying for a nurse to carry on through the day.

I went on duty wondering if I would find my little one there. She was and I was so happy! Her chart was not very encouraging, however, but she was alive and I could still try. I put my hands on her and hummed softly, hoping the sensations could reach her little body. She was not jaundiced and I felt good about that. So we passed another night and she lived through another day. I had two more nights before I would be off for three nights.

I turned her, tried all I knew, wished I could have given her a brandy wrap as I had heard of babies like that responding to brandy wraps—wetting flannelette with brandy and wrapping the infant and just patting the body all over. Here rules were rules.

By the fourth night she seemed to be neither here nor there, but I felt no will to live. Her little organs were

CHAPTER FIVE: *Sojourns in the United States* 113

tired and were giving up. I knew when I left for my nights off that I would not find her there when I returned. I told her I was sorry I could not find a way to help her, but maybe she did not come to stay and I had to release her into that larger life from which she had come.

All the other babies were doing quite well, some better than others, but still showing evidence of staying alive. When I went back on duty, I learned that she had lived one more night. After my four months, I knew that preemie care was too intense for me.

Room 19

While training at the Medical Center I ran into trouble for leaving my unit without permission, but I just had to. My morning assignment was to take care of four patients in the Postoperative unit. I was doing fine until the third patient. While combing her hair, I knew I had to go to room 19. I told the lady I would be right back. When I went down the hall to room 19, I saw an elderly patient that was not ambulatory trying to get out of the bed. I then stopped at the nurse's station to report that the patient in room 19 needed assistance. The charge nurse knew I was assigned to ward 4, so I had no business in room 19. I had no explanation, so she said I should see her when I was through with my patients. I was in trouble!

So, I went back to my task and the same feeling, "go to room 19," came again. So, I made a second trip to room 19. She had almost shuffled off the bed and I realized I could not move her by myself. I asked a nurse to help me get the lady back in the bed. The nurse suggested we put the lady to sit in a chair and we made her comfortable.

I went back to my area. I had finished my work and was doing my charts when the same room 19 message came again. This time the lady was in the chair, but it looked like she was dead. I felt no pulse, so I thought,

"Now I am really in trouble."

I saw some people I presumed to be doctors coming off the elevator. I ran out and asked one of them to look in on the patient. To my great relief, he moved towards the room, then to my dismay he sent me for the charge nurse.

"What are you doing there again? Haven't I told you? You will get into serious trouble if you do this sort of thing."

I really had no explanation that was intelligible to anyone but myself. I could not tell her I got a message out of the blue. They do not believe in those things. She wanted to see me at her desk. She scolded me again. However, she admitted that, though I had no business in room 19, the doctor had said that it was a good thing I called him when I did, for the patient was almost gone when he got there. When I finished my training on the unit, I was relieved that she gave me a very good report.

A Sick Baby

One day I found myself taking care of a very sick infant. The child's grandmother knew the infant was not well but put it down to missing her parents. Her eyes grew bigger and bigger as she grew thinner and thinner and she had no appetite. I was concerned.

I did not want the grandmother to see me take the child, as she would question me. I told her I was going to gas station next door and would be back in a little while. The baby was asleep, which she often was. I wrapped her frail body with plenty of tender loving care and went out through the back door.

I called Unity and told them I had a sick infant in my arms and needed help. The person on the other end answered with an assuring statement. Then she asked if the baby could hear. She could so I was instructed to put the receiver to her ear and the person spoke to her. The baby was now awake. She listened, looked at me and kept looking to see who was talking to her. The talking ceased. About two short affirmations were

CHAPTER FIVE: Sojourns in the United States

spoken. It was like the baby wanted to hear more and she looked at me wonderingly. I spoke similar words to her as I rocked her, trying to give her what I knew to be true. She was in the love of God's creative wholeness.

When babies are very ill, they do not move their toes, but as soon as they begin to feel better, they signal their joy by moving their toes and soon their feet, especially when taking food. I knew that something had been touched, had been reached and there would be a response. Ah, yes, little toes were saying they felt new life, and as she took her bottle those little toes were working away, signaling the body to get going. Toes, feet, up and up through the body were the signs of joy. Her colour was not yet rosy but that would come.

She could stand up holding on, and then she got the idea of walking and learned to respond to "Come". The day her parents returned, she stood off awhile, then to the urgings of "Come" she laughed and walked to them.

Ernestine Calls

I was ready to go to work and found a good job as a Doctor's Assistant. I was to go around with him on his rounds to senile patients as he had quite a number of them.

Three days before I was to start, I heard as though Ernestine, my old friend in Jamaica, called me three times. I had made a promise to her that I would be with her when she was ready to go on.

I cancelled the arrangements for work and told my friends I had to go to Jamaica. I left shortly after, but I never wrote my friend anything. I just went.

I arrived at the house to find Ernestine sitting in her rocking chair. She was happy to see me and said, "I was just here waiting for you to come. I told the others that you would be here today." She had done so indeed!

A few days later I told her that I wanted to visit some friends. She did not want me to go, but I told her I would not stay long. The second night the family called to say she had fallen and broken her hip. She was 96 and I knew this was it!

We had some very good times together and one day she asked me to sing some hymns for her. Then she said she was hearing beautiful music.

"Listen," she said. "I've never heard music like that before." I told her that music was only for her and she must enjoy it.

Night Supervisor

Some things happen on the journey of life that seem hard to believe. They are like captured dreams that one wants to relive, to examine, to analyse, to have answers for. I needed a job and Charles and Ida Beale, Quakers who lived in Winetka, invited me to stay with them, saying maybe there would be a job at a nearby hospital. It was a research hospital for mental and emotional diseases, so I went to check it out.

The chief said he had need for an Assistant Night Supervisor and I would have to learn the switchboard. I was willing to learn. Then, as an afterthought, he said there was one problem. All the staff were white and I would be the only non-white. The hospital took coloured people as patients, but it was an expensive place, $350 cash or certified check on admission to begin with.

I told him I believed I could handle it and he agreed to give me the job. I learned to use the switchboard and found that some of the night helpers wanted to learn a few skills—how to take blood pressure, do temps, give enemas and learn about oxygen.

They were there to help in emergencies as this place had a wide range of patients with mental and emotional problems, alcoholics, drug addicts, folks with suicidal tendencies, psychotics, schizophrenics, senile patients, and a few patients with post-partem depression.

CHAPTER FIVE: Sojourns in the United States

The settling was wonderful except for winter, as it was on the shore of Lake Michigan. I could live in, too, and that was even better, for being a night nurse—eleven to seven with ten days on and four days off. I was able to do some training in Occupational Therapy if I wanted. Since I realized that I might sometimes want to go on a day shift, I took time to catch up with that offer.

This was some place, but I was not afraid of it. The security and emergency systems were excellent, and I found the staff to be quite pleasant. Many of them were people who had been treated for one thing or another and a few alcoholic breakdowns, but they were all friendly and I was able to do my work without experiencing relationship difficulties.

Several things happened that put me wise to what might happen and how one must be prepared for the unexpected. One very quiet night I answered the switchboard to hear someone calling the doctor on duty. He answered and then came to me somewhat agitated. He needed to go home immediately and would be gone for an hour and a half or so. I failed to ask him who would cover for him, but he did leave a number where I could reach him. He would be 20 minutes away from the hospital.

No sooner had he driven out than a car drove in with a patient in serious condition. I told them the terms for admission and they had come with their cash. I invited them to sit in the waiting room and called my assistant, who was a very sharp man. He said we should admit the man to one of the downstairs examining rooms. We did and I saw that the man looked dehydrated, his vital signs were such that without immediate attention he would probably die.

I tried calling the doctor who calmly told me he had just got in. The patient had to have an I.V. He asked if I could start one and he gave me the timing. He told me what to get and I was to call him to say if things were going right.

But, what about the family? They needed to speak with the doctor. He informed me that he would come when he finished his business at home. It was very important for him to do that. He suggested the family wait until I reported to him.

The male nurse could not start an I.V., but I could and showed him the doctor's instructions and what I had to use. The man was restless so we had to restrain his arms a little. I found the vein, put the needle in and watched the life-giving fluid go through drop by drop. I sent the assistant to tell the family that the man was getting attention and then called him back. I told them myself and suggested they wait a while longer.

I went back, checked the man, and called the doctor. "Keep him there for a half hour and, if he continues to respond, tell them they could see him the next day and I will call them later," he said.

Both the assistant and I felt that would never do, so he said let me go and tell them that he would be all right and would be admitted to the male recovery ward. They were satisfied and left.

The doctor called and I reported. He instructed me to admit him to the ward and have the ward nurse check and report in fifteen minutes and then in half an hour. The man's colour was better and he was quieter but he was still serious. He had been admitted before and was an alcoholic. Usually the family brought him in before he became so dehydrated, but the next day they explained that he had left home and it was only by chance that they heard of his condition and went for him. It took him quite a while to recover sufficiently to leave the hospital. I wondered if he ever realized how near to losing his life he had come.

In the absence of one of the unit nurses, I worked as a unit charge nurse on the day shift. I had to admit patients to the ward, do the charting, and supervise two assistants, one of whom had himself been treated for alcoholism.

CHAPTER FIVE: Sojourns in the United States 119

This was one of the admitting units where observation of the patient was very important. Some believed they were being admitted because their families wanted to get hold of their money. Some refuse to remove hats and gloves. Many refused to give their jewelry up for safe-keeping, and some were downright hostile. Coaxing was no good for that immediately put the patient in a power position. One had to have a store of coping mechanisms and often routine was impossible.

One night a patient came to the desk with a Scrabble game. He wanted someone to play with him. The unit was very quiet and, as the man had been very communicative, I thought I could learn something.

I told him I only could play one game as I had some work to get done. He offered to help me with my work.

"Just lock in everybody and put earplugs in," he suggested. Then he added, "that won't do. They would break the glass windows and escape. That's how I got out of the last hospital I was in, but it would be stupid to try that here because these people are human."

We got on with the game. He said I was good at it and I won. He took his game and went to his room saying he was feeling better. He felt he could sleep and asked if I would play another night. I told him I would if things were quiet.

Many patients liked to come to the desk in the early morning hours and they said all sorts of things. One man told me not to let his wife visit him that afternoon because it was the day he had to kill her.

"Just keep her away today," he said.

I reported the matter and hoped it would be taken seriously for this was a dangerous man. His state of anger could be felt. I was more than shocked when they let her in for a visit. He was in his room and I called the desk to check whether she was to be there.

"Yes," the doctor said, "she can see him."

As soon as she hit that door, he slammed it shut, grabbed her and, if that hospital had not had the emergency system it did, she never would have come out alive. I pushed the buzzers for help from two units and from the desk, and they were able to restrain him. When he was calm some hours later, he asked me to see him. Still restrained and sedated, he was very penitent.

He told me I was to blame because he had asked me not to let her come that day. I listened carefully to this man as he went over what was going on in his mind. He knew that his wife would forever be afraid of him. He really loved her and, if she had been kept away, he might have been cured. He had killed before, but he had not told anyone of his need to do it before the act. The first time he was able to say it, nobody paid any attention to him. He believed I would have, but I did not listen to him. It made no sense to argue my case with him, but I did speak to the Director about it. The man knew he would be transferred to another unit, or maybe to another hospital.

Many questions remain unanswered. He might have turned around and said that the hospital was keeping his wife away. Still, that man had come to the desk and opened himself to reveal a most dangerous state of mind that should have been heeded. I could not understand the hospital authorities. Maybe, instead of the man's further condemnation to a very restrictive mental institution, he might have found his way to his own deliverance that day.

This was the same patient who, two weeks after I was working on the unit, came one night and asked in a very quiet voice,

"Nurse, what church do you belong to:"

I told him and his response was,

"I knew it. I knew it all along."

I was not afraid of patients and they knew it. One man had been an executive, highly educated and very

CHAPTER FIVE: Sojourns in the United States

intense. He did not bother with the other patients and every now and then he would come to the desk, make a statement and go back to his room. I was sorry this trouble happened for his dark place seemed to have been getting lightened up. His wife came to see him regularly and they seemed to be a caring couple. I really wish I could understand events such as this.

As I knew about medicines, I was often assigned to prepare dosages for some patients on drug recovery, I had to go into a special room and lock myself in. One night, as I prepared the medicine. I became aware of someone on the stairs. A woman was there showing me her wrists that were bleeding. I had to think fast. I had telephone access to the desk and I had buzzers to call for emergency help, I continued to do my work and the woman stayed where she was. I felt that she wanted me to open the door and she would attempt to get in and get at some drugs.

I used the buzzer and was relieved to see two aids come for the woman. They waited until I had locked the drug room and was safely on the unit. The woman was not in serious condition and my own belief is that she hoped to lure me into opening the door. She was in for drug addiction and from her records she would probably be there for quite some time.

One night as I made my rounds, I heard someone snoring heavily. I checked the charts and questioned as to who was snoring in a disturbing manner. I was told it was Dr. Jones in Room 9.

"It could not be," I told the nurse, "since the snores are coming from the right. It would have to be an even number.

I asked the nurse to check out the matter and she simply said she knew it was Dr. Jones as he snored that way every night. I made a second request and was ignored. So, I walked down the hallway and found a patient in deep distress. I had to think fast. I needed help, but could not use the unit nurse. I was the night supervisor, but I was coloured, you see. There were two nurses that night, a man and wife but they were not going to obey me.

I instructed her to go to Unit 4 and ask the aid there to come immediately. She went and he came hurriedly. I had been teaching him to take blood pressures, read temps, give enemas, help with oxygen and some emergency procedures.

We raised the foot of the bed and I sent him for an oxygen tank. I called the doctor on call and proceeded to prepare the injection I knew he would give. I had the key to the emergency supplies on the unit and I had learned from previous experience what would be given. If the dosage was incorrect, he would correct it when he got there.

He checked and it was in order, so he gave her the injection. Soon I felt my heart beating fast and I tried to calm myself. Then very slowly I knew she was responding. The doctor thanked me for being on the ball and I thanked my helper.

He wanted to know what happened. I hated to do it, but had to tell him that the couple in the unit had given her an overdose of the tranquilizer. She had been very noisy and the female nurse had given her an additional dose of medicine that was not charted. Her husband then gave a second tablet, so the patient had an overdose though not intentionally.

I never saw them again, but others told me they were seen driving out with their suitcases. They had been involved in giving medicine without authorization on other occasions so they were let out.

I thought of my training at the Indianapolis School of Practical Nursing, which was nationally recognized among the top schools. The Director was very strict, but I never forgot how she used to insist that in good nursing care, nothing is to be taken for granted, hence my own insistence on checking out who was snoring on that night.

CHAPTER FIVE: *Sojourns in the United States*   123

I could not understand why the couple refused to check it out when requested. The patient would probably not get well enough to leave the hospital, but it was my duty to do what was needed to save her from dying from an overdose of medicine.

I really did not want to do nursing, but in the moment, I was thankful for the training I had undergone at the Medical Center. I knew that I would not remain there for very long, but the pressure to move away was not yet strong enough, so I carried on learning a whole lot about alcoholics, drug addicts, nervous and emotional diseases, and about humanity without God.

Train to Kentucky

Life in the United States had its ups and downs. I found it hard to remember that there were restroom signs that said "White" and "Coloured". At the airport I found myself in a "white toilet" and was thankful that nobody was around to bother me about it.

The MacFarlands had invited me to visit them in Russell Springs, Kentucky. I also wanted to see a cousin of mine who was living in Louisville. Through me, the MacFarlands had sponsored my cousin to come to the States.

When I got on the train going to Kentucky, I saw a vacant seat and calmly sat in it. The lady next to me was weeping bitterly and I just had to ask her what was wrong. She told me she was taking her husband's body home to Ohio. They had lived in Miami for sixteen years. He died quite suddenly and she was not sure what she would do. She seemed glad to have me talking with her and though I realized that I was on an all-white train, I just sat it out. I was light-skinned and my hair was straightened, so I guess they were not sure of my category.

It was an uneventful journey to Kentucky. The train stopped in Jamestown and I was to transfer to a bus leaving for Russell Springs. It snowed and snowed and got very cold. By the time I got to Jamestown all traffic by road to Russell Springs had ceased. The roads were icy and the wind was strong. I got off and this time I found myself in a waiting room for coloureds. It was not heated so I sat there shivering. I learnt that there was no traffic to my destination and the telephone lines were down.

The mailman, a white man in his sixties, had to pick up and send the mail on each train, so he stopped by to see what I was doing. He told me that the train station would only stay open until midnight, so I was back in the same situation as when I slept next to the wall in Jamaica.

I had my little talk with God. For one thing, I was freezing and for another I had to leave soon. The little man was concerned and told me that someone was coming to pick him up and he would ask him to take me to the Greyhound station that stayed open all night. He said his friend was anti-coloured, but he would ask him anyway. I thanked him and waited.

After a while I heard them coming. The other man, a young, well-built person, took my two suitcases and we left the station. He was quite pleasant and I was sure the fact that I was not American was a big help.

He asked if I was hungry. He said he could not take me into the restaurant because of the colour thing, but that he would buy it and we would eat together in the car. So I asked for a cup of coffee and a sandwich. We all sat in the car eating. They asked where I was from, so I told them I had come up from Jamaica, but I belong to British Honduras. They asked a lot of questions and I told them I was a missionary. They were very nice, though. They took me to the Greyhound station and bought my ticket to Russell Springs. The young man gave me $20 and the old man gave me $10. I was grateful. I got his address and the name of his friend. He left wishing me well.

The station was warm and I had to stay until 9:30 the next morning, but the weather was better and I got to Russell

Springs in fine shape. I called my friends who came to pick me up at the station. It was good to be in the MacFarlands' home where I could stay for three weeks of rest.

Brother Charles

Mrs. MacFarland was very concerned that I did not have a husband and set about introducing me to some coloured friends of theirs. The two coloured brothers were quite wealthy. Their parents had left them the 140-acre farm. They said their father had worked for a rich white family. When one of them died, they gave him this 140 acres because he had been such a good person working for them. The brothers had horses, cattle, and sheep. Brother Charles was a tailor who sewed for white people. He told me all about how many sheep he had and everything.

My cousin had come from Louisville and we all went there in the evening. As we came into the house, I saw a nice room with a beautiful bedspread and fresh flowers. Brother Charles said, "Since our mother died, we keep her room just like this and we put fresh flowers in there every week."

Their big house also had a room where he did his sewing, a big living room with piano, kitchen and dining room. And then upstairs, there were more bedrooms.

Mrs. MacFarland told them I played the piano, so I played and we sang some hymns until I got tired. Then we went home.

The next day my cousin and I went to their church, a little broken-down coloured church in Kentucky. It was shameful how the coloured churches were all broken down there in Kentucky. The MacFarlands did not go with us. They went to the Friends Church.

There were about fifty people in that little church. Brother Charles got up and said,

"I have been praying to the Lord to send me a partner and this good friend told me she knew just the right person."

All the people were clapping and saying, "Alleluia! Praise the Lord, Brother Charles! God is good. He had answered your prayers!"

And the parson got up and said, "Congratulations, Brother Charles. Praise the Lord! I sincerely hope that I will be the one to perform this special ceremony."

Brother Charles said, "And best of all, she's a musician." He asked me to play a hymn that I had played the night before. They had an old piano there.

I was never so embarrassed. I could have died! I knew nothing about this. We had never talked about love or marriage or anything. Mrs. MacFarland never told me anything either. It was very bad! How was I going to tell this man I did not want any of that?

After church my cousin and I went with those two for a picnic by a lake. They brought all the food, very nice food. We never talked about courting or anything. Then they took us back to the MacFarlands' house. He never heard from me again. He wrote me a letter and sent a present, a little cheap bracelet, but I never answered.

Mrs. MacFarland told me I had broken the man's heart. But I told her, "You can't promise me to any man. How am I going to get up every morning and feed sheep? And, I would have to keep up that room for their mother, too! You shouldn't do a thing like that and not even tell me."

Whenever my cousin comes to Belize to visit, we always remember that story and laugh together.

Carmel Meeting

The colour question became most difficult in 1957 when I tried to establish myself as a part of a Quaker Meeting. While I was in nurses training, I often went to visit Evelyn and Marcus Kendall on weekends. Because I was in Carmel with them, I went to the Friends Church there.

CHAPTER FIVE: Sojourns in the United States

True, I was the only coloured person attending the church, but I knew lots of people in the church and they seemed very friendly. I was new there and they had those little cards you fill out if you are new to the church. You fill out a little card if you would like to reach Sunday School, sing in the choir, or apply for membership.

My friends said, "why don't you fill out the card? Then it will go to Ministry and Council."

I filled out the card and marked three things, including membership. But nothing happened. Evelyn said to me, "Are you sure you put it in?"

She and her husband were on Ministry and Council and they knew it had not come up there.

I said, "yes, I put it in the offering plate just like you said."

"Fill out another one," said Keith and Autumn Cox, who also belonged to Ministry and Council.

I filled out the second one and still nothing happened. They wanted to question it, but I said,

"Don't bother. I don't want you to bother. Don't ask any questions. Just leave it like that."

I was not disappointed or troubled by this because I did not plan to make my home there. It proved to me that colour was not accepted there. I was the only coloured one at Carmel Meeting, but not being American, I could be considered in a different way. The only coloured people who came to Carmel worked as maids. None lived there. There is no doubt there was prejudice. Those small communities were all white. Even if they had the money, coloured people could not buy a house there.

The Kendalls where I stayed were a special family. The girl who came to clean their house was well known to them and respected. They introduced me to her and we chatted. She told me that they were the finest people. When they had lunch they set a place for her at the table with them.

Any time there was a party I went right along. I was a part of the family and that felt good to me. I was accepted because of who the Kendalls were. I remember one time I went to a home that was having something for the church. The Kendall daughters told me later that was the first time any non-white person had been in that home.

For a while I had a private job in Carmel, taking care of Mrs. Elliot, Mrs. Kendall's mother, who was almost blind. I'll never forget the day someone told her I was coloured. She said to me, "I've got a question. Are you a darkie?"

I answered, "I am a coloured person, not from America, but from Belize, British Honduras. In Belize we have black, white, Spanish, English, all kinds of people living there and everybody gets along. We don't have the colour question like you have here. We don't have any 'darkies.'" She did not make any fuss.

Then thirty-five years later, in 1992, Carmel Meeting invited me to come for a week when they were having a special program on missions. They paid passage and everything. When I finished speaking, they came up with this piece of paper and said that Carmel meeting would like to invite me into membership in that meeting. They knew I had no membership in any Friends meeting and they would like for me to be a member of Carmel Meeting. And I just thought how the ball rolled, how God works in mysterious ways. I was not going to ask for membership because I never felt I needed it. I felt like I could move around and membership was not important. The next year I was recorded as a Minister in Western Yearly Meeting.

Earlham School of Religion

I wanted to go to Earlham School of Religion because I felt like I needed that training to do my work here in Belize. No one else asked for it. Only I felt it. I was able to go through the financial support of United Society of Friends Women. Maxine Bean arranged for that.

CHAPTER FIVE: Sojourns in the United States

I really wanted to improve my theological education. I function at a certain level, but then there is the regular theological thinking that I was introduced to by going there. It raised a lot of questions in me, some of which still trouble me.

The classes were formal with lots of reading. I found it very difficult to do all the reading and library work. I had not done that for some time. It was hard, but I managed to keep up. I especially enjoyed Dr. Miriam Burke's classes on spiritual growth and development.

It was also hard because of cultural differences. I found I had a different understanding of some of the Bible. Kenneth Hall from Jamaica was also there and he said the same thing. The way they think about certain things up there, we do not think about it that way.

We have a different kind of faith. The average American grows up in the midst of plenty. Maybe not everyone has a lot, but still they see it all around. But we just know what we call "sufficient unto the day." The average student in that class did not know about sufficient unto the day. They have grown up with planning and thinking that you must know that everything is there for tomorrow.

We did not grow up like that. We got food for the day and when tomorrow comes you will worry about that. That is one reason why I do not worry about tomorrow because of sufficient unto the day. I am going to have enough. In those Jamaica days I did not know how I would live from day to day. I did not have five cents, but yet I knew that I would live through each day and come out as good as ever. That is faith!

But we were heard, so there was no real problem. Otherwise I would have left.

I lived upstairs. It was a privilege because I had quarters to myself. I shared kitchen facilities with the couple downstairs. They laughed at my cooking, but that was all right. It was just a part of the cultural differences.

Speaking to Friends in the US

The very first time I went to Western Yearly Meeting to Indiana I was asked to speak. Afterwards a lady talked to me and I always appreciated her for saying this to me.

"I got some pieces of what you said and I wish I had gotten all of it. If you slow down, you can have a big impact on Americans."

It is from there that I learned to talk to Americans. After I had learned to speak slowly, I had a group and I said, "If you do not understand anything, you ask me to repeat it, because I want you to understand me. I do not want to be here speaking a foreign language."

A man in my group told his wife she should leave the group she was in and come to mine. So, I ended up with a big group.

While I was at Earlham School of Religion, I spoke at a different church each Sunday, and they would give me a little stipend. I enjoyed it the most at the Senior Citizen Home and the people seemed to enjoy it. I would never have thought they would understand because of the differences in my speech. I went the first Sunday and told the biblical story about the woman with the issue of blood. Many of them had never heard it told that way, especially the attention I paid to the descriptive aspect of this woman coming to Jesus, wanting to touch and being afraid to touch. I really made it come alive. They asked me to come back the next Sunday. From then on, whenever I had free time, I went there. I was surprised that the older ladies understood me when some of the younger ones had difficulties. They would come and talk about something I had said that had great meaning for them.

When I am asked to speak, they usually already have a theme, like "Launch out into the Deep". I have

CHAPTER FIVE: Sojourns in the United States

Sadie Vernon in the United States in 1991

life experiences that tie in with the theme, like the time I was coming from North Caicos Island when we were caught in the storm. The man came to us and said we could not wait until tomorrow morning. He was calling us to launch out with this boat so we could get there safely. God had other ideas! He gave me an experience. "Will your anchor hold in the storms of life?" When we finally found a clump of mangrove, he threw the anchor into the roots and it held through the storm.

I have spoken in many places in the U.S. and they gave me a freedom to say some big things to them. They really listened to me. They accepted my terms and most of them left with something they had not heard before, but it answered questions they had in their minds. I know that I have an impact there. A lot of people tape my speeches. I think that I am saying some old things in a new way. I recently got a letter from someone talking about somethin I said in a speech in Greensboro. That was a long time ago and she still remembers. Here are two of those speeches:

Ministering to a Different World

Friends, first of all my greetings from my home country Belize and then my thanks for your invitation to think with you on this extremely important consideration of ministering to a different world.

Often in my journeys among you, we have taken sweet counsel together, we have challenged and encouraged others. We have dreamed great dreams of our call to be faithful as members of the Society of Friends and now we seem to be saying that what seemed to be friendly old states of consciousness are no longer enough for this day and age.

Of course, we sense new directions that call for changes and I believe that because of the fantastic claims we make about our particular way of thought and life we are now being put on the line to prove it.

Someone sent me a volume called "The Year 2001" another sent me the "Global 2000" report, and I have received many booklets on the coming world situation. What thought and planning have been done by secular agencies! These documents were sure of a few things.

There will be more people living in misery at the end of the century than now. There will be more than 25 million refugees; more than half the world's people will still be illiterate; the age of motherhood will continue to fall; and there will be many more polygamous relationships and single parents. Islam with no economic power will, along with other religions, become an increasing challenge to our assumptions. There will be drastically reduced giving to world relief and to missions.

All the religious ones suggest that all Christian denominations must take stock. A different world has already been taking shape and we are well into a whole generation of it. If by now we have not recognized that and have not planned our ministries around it, we are late.

The World Council of Churches had a man by the name of Visser t'Holt working in the missions department.

CHAPTER FIVE: Sojourns in the United States

He believed that life is a perpetual examination and God the examiner. Take Jesus Christ—was he not constantly tested, sort of always being up against it in family, society, faith, and is he not set as the plumb line?

Your theme led me to wonder if you were not like the mother of James and John. Or, as Mark puts it, they asked the questions themselves. They did not really know what they were asking but once they said "we are able", their request was granted and you and I have their story. So, they still minister to us and confront us. We are urged when we ask for "ministry to a different world" to first answer how have we been doing it to date. Now that the different world has rocked the boat and we are face to face with the urgency to really be about the Father's business.

Before I go on, I want to know that all of us here and every member of the meetings and world wish that every member of the Society of Friends is saying "we are able" for whatever their ministry calls us to be about. Surely you already know the price you have to pay. What will really count in the long run is not your activities, nor your intellectual pursuits, for the line is drawn and begins with your commitment to God.

The history of mankind and indeed of civilization shows that 90 percent of human effort went into survival. Because of science and technology, particularly in the area of communications, the world has moved from village culture to cosmopolitan and now to the planetary which we can hardly comprehend. I read recently that we receive some 65,000 pieces of input daily and for most of the world that is creating an overload we have not been trained to handle.

For one thing, we have to learn the vast difference between conceiving and perceiving. Everywhere we are experiencing severe breakdowns in family structure and as I listen to people who come for counselling, I see two very serious elements—submission and domination.

How does one minister to this kind of crisis? And, it is more common than we believe. We have to understand the how and why of it and often we come at it with "Let's pray about it" when we know not how to answer. That might be a sort of beginning but we, especially Quakers, can see that our people must be helped to understand what communion has to do with consummation. How does that happen when there is a strong sense of the others? Surely, we must increase our capacity for creativity, for exploring the riches of ourselves and of each other. This world crisis calls us to help in the creation of the new humanity.

Humanity in general seems to want the right to destroy old structures and to create new ones. It seems that loneliness, alienation of self and selfhood do not lessen in spite of new dimensions of our time. As was discussed at the gathering on Missions and Evangelism held by the World Council of Churches last year in Texas, human beings have become mechanized, routinised, and made comfortable as an object, with the result that they have been displaced and thrown off-balance as a subject. So, we must deepen our ministry of reconciliation and be certain of what the Gospel means to the deep sense of alienation.

We listened to people who were experiencing revolution, but also to the search for social conditions of humanity. Once people were resigned to poverty as their lot, that was true no more. Rising expectations continue everywhere. Social iniquities and oppression were once accepted. Not so today! And, there is a strong consciousness of fundamental rights of individuals, even of children.

We find a growing sense of common humanity and solidarity leading to mutual concern and Christians are deeply involved in these struggles. There was a whole lot to be said on the issue of secularism and there was great defensiveness against it, particularly from Europeans. All of us non-Catholics were written off and out of the kingdom by some of the diehards, who informed us that the Holy Spirit could only be mediated through their

CHAPTER FIVE: Sojourns in the United States

liturgy. So, the evangelical left the group and there was heightened defence by those of us considered lost sheep.

Secularism has now developed a total philosophy and way of life, so world religions have ceased to be a significant factor in the life of millions who were once religious.

I believe it was Tillich who said "True communication of the Gospel means making possible a separate decision for or against it." I heard that at a conference and am trying to find out where the quote came from.

We must also look at the structures. Often churches are set up with structures designed for conservation. This idea must go. The Church must indeed be the community of the new age. The pilgrim people demonstrate the powers of the ages.

For a long, long time the Church was a place to go to hear the Gospel. For three centuries there were no permanent structures. Believers met whenever there was opportunity for worship, witness, and service. The great major change came in the fourth century when the state adopted the church and the church became comfortable and felt the need for permanence. In the eighth through tenth centuries, social patterns shifted and communities became stable enough to establish the parish system of settled clergy.

For more than a thousand years it went on until the nineteenth and twentieth centuries when world unrest began. Mobility became easier and easier and old structures had to be examined until today we have mega-churches.

Friends were caught in this and in many places felt the need to move from simple meetinghouses to larger complexes as modern as that word can mean to Friends. We know that at our best we can work cooperatively and tenderly with the in-dwelling Spirit that fills all creation.

What we have from Jesus Christ is timeless. Every age and generation have had to make its own significant discovery. He dealt with some matters that are relevant to the existing conditions in the social order of this time—divorce, almsgiving, politics. But always He was moving the social order towards the ideal, not merely a good life, but a spiritual life. His commitment to God and His measure of fellowship give evidence of a creative moral power—new values, new insights.

I have great concern for what our children and youth are learning from us. I never cease to wonder how much our children are already in the new age, seeking and seeing in new ways that never occurred to me when I was a child.

(Indiana Yearly Meeting, August 1990. Courtesy of Maxine and Elmer Featherston)

A New Departure from Old Ways

The world has taught us that we must have a comprehensive plan, something reasoned out that has logical conclusions. We hear a lot about the end of the century and all big businesses have already worked out their ten-year plans. Governments usually talk about a five-year plan as that is the lifespan of a party—five years at a time. People with less income go at it every three years and some annually.

So, many of these long-term things admit that they did not work out according to plan, like the General Agreement on Tariffs and Trade (GATT), the UN Conference on Trade and Development (UNCTAD). These UN attempts are always breaking down and starting over. UNICEF (United Nations International Children's Emergency Fund) has been a very stable one, mainly because it deals with life and with the coming generations, from the starting place.

We are always trying to upstage Jesus Christ. The story, the symbols, the images of things new and old, were all offered, but his basic message centred around his faith. What we really see is how he showed us a way to deal with recurrent problems, whether class, race, or creed.

CHAPTER FIVE: Sojourns in the United States 137

The goals he set for all who wanted to be kingdom people are as valid today as they were when first given.

Testing, trials, pressures, endurance from one part of ministry in any age. But there is also hope and joy because when we are faithful in ministry, we will be able to say with Jesus, with Paul, and all the hosts of witnesses, that we have kept the faith.

Does this ministry call to private as well as public proclamation of the faith? What clear answers do we have for today's world? There can be no observing of the message of social justice, there must be a universal interpretation of Christianity.

As we go to our deepest level of thought for an answer to how to minister to the world of today, we are aware that when the social and economic conditions of life are radically changed, there has to be a radical reinterpretation of religion.

We are today dealing with several generations that have had a great feeling of pride in what has been achieved. A great number of people want to hear nothing about eternal life. It seems that we have great difficulty in making people believe that we belong to a new world society that is inclusive. Are we talking about transformation of society? Are we clear as to what we see ahead, what is the potential outcome of ministry? We have to be sure that we are in harmony with this ongoing good purpose God has for the world.

I hear this Yearly Meeting issuing a summons for a new departure from old ways of doing things, old programs, and old formulas that are not working. You seem to have called yourselves to account for what and how you have done things. You have found yourselves wanting and so feel the urgency for a departure from old ways of doing.

Whenever this happens it is because we have come to new discoveries about ourselves and our places in the scheme of things. This discovery pushes us into fresh insights about humanity, about God, and about all of life. Friends have always been a thinking people, and to live with the conventional and the traditional is not enough. In our best moments, we have known how to yield and how to stand firm. Now and then we even enter into serious acceptance of the Science of being. So, we have kept in touch with the wellsprings of life and our churches and meetings have understood that our call is to a way of life. Surely, we have always seen and known God as presence and power, as wisdom and love, as the all and we are the part.

Do we know that we are called to minister in a way that leads to transformation and, as scripture says, "by the renewing of the mind"?

There was a time when I believed that the evangelization of my country belonged to the missionaries, but long, long ago, my generation realized that was not true. Unless we were allowed to be involved in the process, the result would be destructive to the future. We were not encouraged to participate at the deepest level—always on the fringe—not seen as agents to be taught and trained by God's spirit with the help of the missionaries.

Some were encouraged not to even think about becoming ministers or missionaries, but because of this dynamic known as the "CALL", many of us continued to believe in ourselves and to make the internal moves necessary. It is so true that the process is from within to without and all of us who kept the faith without a call have found God faithful to bring it about.

You have felt a new call to meet the challenges presented by a new world that has evolved into its present form by the atomic and space ages.

You are therefore feeling God's pressure on your commitment to God's design and purpose for the world. You have thought and probably fought your way through to principles and polices demanded by this new world situation. Now you are ready for a new and bold adventure. (Indian Yearly Meeting, August, 1990)

CHAPTER FIVE: Sojourns in the United States

Return to British Honduras

I came to the end of my days as a student at the School of Religion and received my degree as Master of Ministry on June 6th, 1976. I did not know what was next, but I was given the go ahead to return to British Honduras. I was in a very quiet frame of mind as I sat down to ponder the future. It was early morning. I knew I went into a doze, but I was looking at a beautiful green field that stretched as far as the eye could see.

Suddenly there was a loud clap of thunder and I was split in two with half falling on the right and half on the left. I was still there looking at the two halves, but now I had no body. I was a glorious ball of light—a circle of atoms of light. I could see and hear and, as I thought of trying to put the two pieces together, a voice said, "You are finished with that now. Leave that and just go forward. You will go north, south, east, and west."

Then I was myself again in my same old body. Now, what was that all about: Old things were sure passed, but this living ball of light—colourful, alive, sensing, seeing, hearing. Maybe I was in a body that could not experience.

Maybe I was being helped to know that there will be a day when there will be no further use for the body and the reality of me will be like the centre of light. Maybe when I go, it will come like a thunderclap and I will be no more. I surely hope that if it comes that way, I will have already known all about it.

Chapter Six
Belize
(1960–2008)

In this kind of work you cannot have a one-track mind. You have to be prepared to do whatever is needed. Life is full of such a variety of experiences, some good, some bad. If I met a millionaire, I would spend out his money in two weeks for poor people.

From this Valley They Say You are Going

It was 1951 before I made my first trip home to British Honduras, ten years after I had left for Trinidad. On this visit home, I stayed for only two months and then went back to Jamaica. British Honduras seemed like a dead end to me then, compared to all that was going on in Jamaica. It was just a vacation. I was not ready to come back home yet.

My grandmother was still alive then and I was really glad to see her. The day I was leaving she asked the radio station to play this song for me.

> *From this valley they say you are going*
> *I will miss your bright eyes and sweet smile*
> *For they say you are taking the sunshine*
> *That has brightened my path for awhile.*

CHAPTER SIX: *Belize*

Going Home

After I completed my nurse's training in the United States in 1960, I moved back to British Honduras because my Aunt Annette was getting old and she wanted me to help in her school. She had retired from playing the organ but still had the school. She expected me to live with her in the house on Racecourse Street. She had always looked upon me as her child, which did not please me at all.

She said, "I know that we can't all live in the old house, so I am building a little house for the two of us."

She was hoping that I would take over her school. But my other aunt, Lena, who had been there through thick and thin at this school, violently objected to my presence in the school. She would not even give me a class to teach. She was used to teaching three classes at once. She had her system. I saw that without Lena, Annette could not have accomplished all that she did. I did not want to break that up, so I worked at the school only part time. The rest of the time I worked at the YWCA.

By that time an awakening had taken place in Belize. They were ready to hear new things. I think John Wesley's greatest contribution was that he accepted ecumenicism as an important direction for Christianity. He recognized it even before the people were aware, but they were ready. That is why Methodism was so successful.

Change must happen. It is a basis of the Christian faith. But people have to be made ready for change. Readiness is a very important thing. It is a waste of time trying to put things over before the people are ready. Even in teaching if a child is not ready—something is missing—a teacher must attend to the readiness.

Christian Social Council

The Christian Social Council had started in late 1957 as a committee. Reginald Helfrick of the Church World Service helped in the beginning. Then there were three churches involved: Presbyterian, Methodist and the Salvation Army. The ecumenical movement was new then. It was important because neither the government nor the individual churches were providing any social services, but the churches working together could.

Mr. and Mrs. Meador came from the United States to help the Council get organized. They were Methodists, but very open-minded. I was working at the YMCA when they came here and they lived at the Y where the Council had an office.

Mr. Meador had worked in a cloth-making factory in the USA and had access to lots of cloth. He had the cloth experience and his wife was into sewing. The Seventh Day Adventist helped them to buy fifteen sewing machines with the other churches. It was the first thing they had done with any other church.

Hurricane Hattie

During Hurricane Hattie I was at my Aunt Annette's school on Racecourse Street along with twenty-one other people, including some older people. We decided we should move to her house because it was new. We tied a rope between the school and the house and all the people, even the older ones, moved safely to the house. After the eye of the storm passed, the wind was behind us, so it was safe to open the door and watch from the porch. The children and I watched the tidal wave with all the cars and everything else floating. We were nine feet high, so we were safe. As in the 1931 hurricane, my Granny's house came off the pillars but it was not damaged otherwise.

Chapter Six: Belize

Hurricane Hattie damage (top); Hurricane survivors in line for relief supplies (*Courtesy Belize National Archives*)

The Council had just started this sewing training program when Hurricane Hattie came. It was the Meadors who had gotten all those blankets and clothing of all description to serve poor people. We had no idea there would be a hurricane. It had all been supplied for the work with the poor. All this was stored in a warehouse at the Fort by the sea. When we heard the hurricane was coming, we moved it all to the YWCA, the same building that exists today. That building was tacked up to the ceiling. Because it was far away from the seaside, the building was not damaged.

So, we never had to send out a call for clothing—it was already here. The YWCA became a hurricane relief centre where people came to get food and clothing. There were families living upstairs and downstairs was for storage of relief supplies, so we had no space for any Y programs. That period after Hurricane Hattie was not a satisfying one for me. It was really backbreaking work. I worked at the YWCA in hurricane relief for five months, until I was completely worn out. Then I went to the US for a rest and stayed with the Kendalls.

Ecumenical Movement

The Meadors wanted me to come back to work here, so the Council offered me the post of Executive Secretary in 1963, when I was still in the US. Before assuming this work, I went travelling to study ecumenical programs in Barbados, Jamaica, Mexico, and the Bahamas.

While in Jamaica I worked for a few months with their Council of Churches. I used to go out to Jonestown, a poor area outside of Kingston. The parents asked if I could get a preschool going, so we did. I also taught classes—handicraft, sewing, and cake decorating. It was a good experience for me because the women were very eager to learn.

One of the women in the group had a daughter getting married, but wedding cakes were very expensive. She could not afford to have one made. So, the group

Chapter Six: Belize

decided to make a five-layer cake for her. The group knew how to make the black cakes in different sized tins. Then we set up the cake at the wedding house. You need four poles to put the second layer above the first and on up to the fifth layer. The group was completely reliable, everybody bringing what they were assigned to bring. That cake was quite the talk of the town for a long time afterward!

The Meadors stayed until I came back and then they left in October of 1963. At first, the Council had an office in a little room off the veranda at the YWCA. The next year we heard about the house on Allenby Street that was available for rent. The Committee agreed that this would be a good area in which to start this work. The YWCA was on the north side of Belize City and there was nothing on the south side. So they rented the building and a year afterward they bought it.

The ecumenical movement was necessary at that time to open doors. The churches were really separated. Even for funerals Catholics would stand outside the Cathedral because they were forbidden to go inside any other church.

The Catholics were not involved in the beginning of the Christian Social Council, but Catholic people began to get involved. Social services of the Council, especially after Hurricane Hattie, really brought people together. We offered classes and other activities that were open to anyone. A lot of Catholics came. So the Catholics who were involved went back and told the Father what we were doing. Eventually the Catholics decided to become members. It was a big decision because they had to provide financial support.

As a leader I could get people together, women especially. I was a representative at a World Council of Churches Conference. That is where I learned about what was going on with women. I went back home and started Church Women United. The women really rallied. Nobody felt put out.

We had ecumenical services in different churches and they all attended, so that got them over the separation. The first week in January was a week of Prayer for Christian Unity. We had services in different churches each night and closed with a big service at the Courthouse Plaza. Church Women United organized a service on the first Friday in March for World Day of Prayer. Each year we went to a different church. For Good Friday and Pentecost there were big services at the Courthouse Plaza with combined choirs singing from the veranda. In November was Christian Council Week and we had a big sale of handiwork. We travelled to visit some rural place, such as, Hattieville, Burrell Boom, or Gracey Rock, and had a service. We could all work together and pray together even though we believed different things.

Belmopan Hostel

At the time of Hurricane Hattie Belize City was the capital of British Honduras, but the hurricane nearly flattened the whole city and it was not expected to recover. So, the officials decided to move the capital further inland, to make a new city called Belmopan. After the government moved to Belmopan, the Prime Minister, George Price, was concerned about housing for the young civil servants that had to go back and forth from Belize City for work. In the planning for the new city, they had forgotten to build housing for them. There were not too many, only seventeen of them. So, he asked if I could do a hostel for them and I got the Council to agree. He said he would put five houses at my disposal, completely furnished and pay all the expenses. I got some of my stalwart helpers from the Council to go with me, five of them. We went up there by truck every day because there was no proper transportation in those days. We wore long boots because we were working in pure mud. We set up the hostel with living, dining and sleeping quarters. The people were wonderful! Everybody was in good spirits. We kept the hostel for a year until adequate housing was in place.

CHAPTER SIX: Belize   147

Mina Grant Centre

One of the first projects was the Mina Grant Centre, which included a government preschool and a day care centre managed by the Council. Mina Grant was a woman from British Honduras who was interested in social work, especially the welfare of children. She was active in the British Honduras Federation of Women, which was a great movement here in the 1950s. But their leadership got old and they did not recruit younger women. They owned a building behind the Majestic, where they allowed the Christian Social Council to start a day care centre.

Belize Continuation School

One of the largest contributions of the Council was the Continuation School We never had any idea that the Continuation School would be the way it turned out, no idea! I am the one that got the seed sown for twenty people. Four mothers came to me and said,

"We cannot get our children into any school. Will you please start something? Miss Sadie, we know you could start something. Start anything and we will support you."

So I sat down and wrote up a project for twenty girls with home economics including general education. YWCA was willing to let us do it there. The proposal was on my desk when Church Women United visited in 1963, right after I had started at the Council. They asked,

"Have you got anything going for girls?"

"Right here!" I could say, because I had this project written up, not knowing where I would send it.

They looked at it and said, "Well, you have a place. We will pay for you to get a home economics teacher."

There was nobody available here at the time but I knew I could get Mrs. Haggith McCalla from Jamaica because she had written me saying that she would like to visit British Honduras. She was a home economics teacher who had just retired. They said,

"We would pay her fare and her salary for one year. Let us know what that is."

And that is how the thing started, with the twenty girls at the YWCA in April of 1964. It was a joint project between the YWCA and the Christian Social Council with Church Women United providing the first funds because the people did not have money to pay. In those days lots of things were much, much cheaper in British Honduras than they are today but still people did not have money to pay the $20 a month for fees. When I was in high school, my fees were $3 a month. Then there was a different set of financial circumstances. The Council did not have churches who could give the money either and you could not go to the government in those days. You had to get your funding from external sources. The fees remain the same in 1998, although the Government of Belize provides support and the families of the students pay fees. The fees have been kept the same for 35 years to make the school accessible to everyone.

Before the next year, the mothers of these girls came and said,

"The girls are coming home with their home economic things, things that we do not know how to do. We wonder if you could set up a class for us to learn some of these things."

So we started an evening home economics class. We had about forty people in each group and the lady from Jamaica was excellent! She really taught them. So, that is how we got it all started, never knowing that we could pull it off. And we could never stop it, so the school kept on growing.

We had a lot of support. Christian Aid paid the salaries for the teachers for five years. Then OXFAM, a British organization, supported it for five years. And then the Primate's Fund from the Anglican Church of Canada gave for five years. The Dutch funded it for two years. It grew by leaps and bounds. By 1982 we had ninety-two students.

Chapter Six: Belize

We stayed at the YWCA until we ran out of space. Then the Catholic priests said, "We do not use our extension building in the daytime, so you could use it. You are doing something that we haven't got set up and we don't intend to start. So, you use the building in the daytime and then do your home economics for adults at the YWCA in the evenings."

The Continuation School was very important. The women learned all these fancy things. Many of them still remember those days. They remember how it all started when women got into learning. They are always coming back to me and saying,

"Maybe we could start this thing."

I say "I can't start another thing. I have done my share. Make somebody else do it now."

They say, "but they won't do it the same way. You know how to do it, how to get it off the ground."

They are at loose ends and a lot of them want to be occupying their time in learning—cake decorating, sewing.

We have been trying to find a permanent place for the Continuation School.

The Methodists offered us some space in the area where Trinity Methodist Church is now. We raised $5,000 and filled the site. Then the Methodist minister changed and the new minister did not know anything about the agreement. We had never drawn up any papers so we had no legitimate claim.

The Presbyterians offered us a whole lot for a lease of $300 a year if we could give them an office in the building. A Peace Corps volunteer made a beautiful plan for us. We planned a good Home Economics unit there. They would learn to cater and to wait tables. They would have offered the public small dinners, whatever you wanted for the menu you could have. But that plan fell through because there was concern that the school would disturb the neighbors.

The government promised us the youth hostel instead, but they did not win the 1993 election, so that plan was high and dry. Then we were given a piece of land at three miles on the Western Highway. The plan was for a school development out there—a primary school, a high school, infant school, nursery school, kindergarten, all in one compound on a big piece of land. They called it the school district. A lot of people have land out there for a whole new settlement. They had a nice plan, but the land was low and could not be built on for two years after they filled it.

In 1994 we leased a building on Dean Street and had more space, so we increased the enrollment to 250. On September 6, 1999, I was honoured in a ceremony in which the Continuation School was renamed "Sadie Vernon High School." At that time Cordele Hyde, Minister of Education, announced that the Sadie Vernon High School would finally have a permanent home on Mahogany Street.

Community Development in St. Martin de Porres

Another highly successful Council project was in St. Martin de Porres, a new development in Belize City. Eva Middleton and myself with Dorothy Rozga of UNICEF gave home economics and arts and crafts classes out there, instead of them having to come all the way to the Council. We had sewing; we had childcare; and UNICEF backed us up with costs.

Then Dorothy said, "Let's do this as an interministerial thing. Let's see if it will work."

So she got three ministries involved, Ministry of Health, Social Services, and Education. That was at the beginning of St. Martin de Porres. Because it was a new area, the roads were not paved. We had to wade through mud and water, but it was very successful. The desire for learning was so great out there.

Neil Snarr from Wilmington came visiting and we were having a macramé class. He said he never got over

CHAPTER SIX: Belize

what people would do to learn. It was a small room and there was not even enough room for everyone to sit down. Some were standing up learning macramé with their hands over the next one's head, everyone trying to learn within a limited space.

Then a wonderful thing happened. I went to a public thing at the park and the Chief Education Officer came to me and said,

"You are working out at St. Martin de Porres? We have tried several other things but then we went out there and saw your project. Do you think you could organize something if we fund it?

I like to do things like that, if someone provides the money. So, I said

"I will see what we can do. I'll send you a plan."

He said, "We have the money and we'll pay the whole cost of it, but we have to spend it before October."

This was March. So, I went to Eva and said,

"Eva, girl, money! Money on the line. Let's go to town."

So we sat down and wrote up a child-care project. We had a little daycare centre called the Pine Street Preschool, a small sewing group, and a centre for cookery. Then we got the bright idea. Why not use the Y? So, we talked to the Y people and they agreed. We set up the Human Development Centre, a joint project between the Council, the YWCA, and the government. That was one of our biggest successes. We gave certificates and everything!

Some of the mothers had to drop out because their men came home at five o'clock and wanted them at home. They could have come to earlier classes or night classes, but they had to drop out. I never thought that would have to happen, but they said,

"Yes, it does happen that way."

And those who could not read began to use their children's school books. One lady came and said her child came home and found her stumbling over this school book, so she told us of her embarrassment. We showed them ways of not embarrassing themselves.

I said, "You don't have to feel bad. After they go to sleep, you could use the books."

They learned more and more. It was a very successful group. Those girls would tell me that they used to wash the dishes and then read Mills and Boone, a book of romantic stories, and go to sleep.

When they were doing the evaluation and we asked them how this had made a difference. A lot of them put it down this way.

"Now we know how to do things, to do crafts."

They were all ages, over 18. We tried to include those under 18, but there were too many over 18. I am sorry we did not have a program for the younger ones. They did not have high school like there is now. We decided to focus on the older ones because they already had homes and were mothers.

I saw them talking about using a box and putting foil over it—solar cooking. A Peace Corps Volunteer taught them. They tried it and they agreed that it would work. But they could not use it because it took too long. The women needed to get dinner ready for twelve o'clock.

Some of them were mothers and had left school long ago. There were such bright people in that group. They picked up their learning skills and trained for the Rural Society of Arts (RSA), a British exam. And some of them got maths and English and a few got typing. They have never forgotten that part of their learning. Just when they thought everything was over, they began again. Some got into preschool teaching, something they would never have gotten into had they not had this particular training program. We had 125 finish the courses, but maybe ten or twelve dropped out. That was an amazing thing.

CHAPTER SIX: Belize

There was one girl that passed the RSA. She was twenty-six years old, had four children, and was not married. She came to me and said,

"You know, Miss Vernon, I always wanted to be a nurse. Like how I have these two certificates, you think they will give me a chance?"

I said, "Don't write yourself off. Apply! Let them tell you no. You don't tell yourself no." She applied and one day she came to the office and said, "I'm going for an interview. But maybe they will ask me about my family."

I said, "Carry those certificates that you have. Carry the ones from the course and from the RSA exam. They will realize that you left school when you were sixteen because you got pregnant and now you have picked up the pieces at this age. Yes, you go ahead!"

She came back afterward saying, "I think I'll make it, you know."

And she did! She got into nursing and when the capping was to be, she came to tell me. She's a full nurse now. But it goes to show you, how many more could have picked up the pieces, but they write themselves off. I always tell people,

"Don't write yourself off because nine of ten times you will get what you're after."

Some of the girls learned how to handle a meeting, how to start up and to give a vote of thanks. I said, "Now you write that thing out."

The refrigerator was right there by where she was standing up, I said, "You put that paper up there on the refrigerator." She got off to a bold start and then she looked at me and I knew what had happened. She had forgotten in midstream, but she had her paper, and she managed to get through it. They had not learned things like that.

A lot of women that went through those classes became preschool teachers. They went on to take teacher's certificates. They got into all sorts of things.

They had ambitions that their dreams could be fulfilled. There is a woman who is on the City Council right now, Olga Gordon, who was one of that first group from St. Martin de Porres. I saw her the other day and she said,

"I never dreamed I could get into anything like this."

"Well, you had to make the start," I replied.

So, that was a wonderful project. It should be written up as part of the history of St. Martin de Porres because it was from the beginning of the first houses there. But if it were not for UNICEF we could not have done it. Dorothy had the vision and she brought the Ministries into it. They did certain things like the sanitation. They really cooperated. That was really a wonderful thing.

Reconciling Ministries

The Council meant a lot to poor people. It was the only thing they had. People came to the Council with any problem and they had a hearing. If I could do something I did. If I needed to call someone, I did that. In this kind of work you cannot have a one-track mind. You have to be prepared to do whatever is needed. Life is full of such a variety of experiences, some good, some bad. If I met a millionaire, I would spend out his money in two weeks for poor people.

A woman came with a baby wrapped up in a blanket, saying her baby was sick. She was a Catholic, so I called the Father at St. Ignatius and told him there was a lady with a baby that needed baptizing. He told her the baby was dead, but she did not believe him. After baptizing the baby, he took them both to the hospital.

A teen-aged boy came to me very ashamed of himself. He was working and had been giving his mother $10 or $15 a week to put up for him. The particular day he wanted $2 for a school picnic, but she did not have the money. He was so angry that he lashed her with his belt. And now he was ashamed. I gave him the $2 for the picnic, but I told him that lashing his mother was a very serious thing. I took him in the back room and gave him twelve lashes, the only time I ever raised a hand to anyone.

Another woman came running down the street with a small child bleeding from the head. There was blood everywhere and she was screaming, "Police going with me!"

I told her the police were not going with her. She and the child were going to the hospital. When I finally got her settled down, I heard the story. She had been beaten by her husband and she taking it out on her children. She had left a tin of condensed milk in the safe and, when she got home it was gone. The children had drunk it. She was vexed, so she started hitting them with a man's belt. The buckle cut the little boy just above his eye.

I had never lived that way. I knew nothing of that kind of hardship. The Council stood as a landmark organization as long as it continued to consider its main task as helping the poor in distress. Distress is a terrible thing. This woman did not know what to do. She had lost all sense of reasoning.

Church women bring up these kinds of issues. What is the right way for a Christian to deal with the issues of life? The church falls down by not helping. What will the church do when a man no longer has the money to feed his family? Every church should have a social agency where people can come and talk.

Confronting Violence

Anger in charge of the human spirit is to be feared, but the spirt of God can intervene to bring relief. It was a hot, steamy day and I was at a meeting of the Interchurch Committee. As the meeting drew to a close, I could hear voices on the street. Someone was being urged to call me for some crisis intervention or the other.

As soon as the meeting ended, I looked through an east window, and one of the neighbours simply said, "You have to go. A man is beating a woman and the police won't go. It's a machete lashing."

Now I had heard of a machete lashing, but had never seen one. "Why me?" I thought, "What if ...?" I put the question aside and remember a Jamaican friend telling me that in these lover's affairs, it was dangerous for males to intervene, but a female outside the family will not be hurt. I thought about that and decided to go to the house.

My co-worker had a car and I told him what was going on. I asked him to drive me around the corner to the house on the next street. I suggested that he keep the motor going.

We went around and he was willing to go with me inside, but I told him I would try it alone. As I went up the stairs, I deliberately walked so the man could hear someone coming up. The door was not shut and I pushed it and went inside. With blinds for partitions he could see me easily.

He was in a blind rage, hitting a person face down on a bed I could see her body with skin shining from the burns made by the steel as it hit her. She seemed lifeless. That scared me quite a bit but I went to the bedroom door not sure what to do.

Then I called to him quietly, "give me the machete."

He was ready to hit her, but the pause was enough.

"You heard me, give me the machete."

He handed it to me, turned from the bedroom to the dining room, put his arms on the table, put his head on his arms, and started to cry. He lost all power to continue beating once the rage was broken.

"If you had not come, I would have killed her."

"What happened?" I asked him.

It was a bad story. Someone called him at his work to tell him that his woman was at another man's place. He left his job and went to the place where he found her with another man. He got a cab and took her home, made her take off her clothes and ordered her to lie nude face down and he started in.

"You know she's unconscious." I said.

He only knew that the anger he felt was enough to let him just beat and beat and beat. He never said he was sorry for his cruelty and I have often wondered if he ever felt guilty.

She lay there like a dead person. I told him to put on some water and asked if he had Vaseline and alcohol or Bay Rum. Then I told him to leave her alone and I would go for his sister.

All this time there was a big crowd on the street. I do not know what they were expecting, but I walked out and got in the car as my friend was waiting. He was glad to see me and said he was nervous but did not know what to do. I told him how it went and that I needed to go for his sister.

So we drove her around and she took over. She told me she had a time trying to bring the girl around and when she did, she was in terrible agony but had no tears.

"Imagine, all the girl said was, 'It's my fault.'"

She would say no more. His sister believed the beating had affected her mind, so she sent for her mother to take her away.

This is how it ended. Now, I could have let the fear of being hurt keep me from going in. I had to put that aside and just go in, as it was necessary to break the anger.

Attending Death

There was a lady that lived at the end of Racecourse Street named Miss Sarah Jenkins. One day she had said to me, "When I am going, I'm going to send for you."

At 11 o'clock one night someone came for me. When I told them I was going to Miss Sarah, my aunts kicked hell that I was going out in the night. But I had made a solemn promise. She was a member of the Guide of the Holy Name. On Saturdays older members went to sweep out and dust the church. Every Saturday she had faithfully cleaned the church.

The Bishop came and gave her Communion. I told her she had a good life and God will have something good for her whenever he appointed her to go. I put my hand over her hand. I knew not to hold her hand. Otherwise I would get caught in the death grip.

United Church of Christ Support

The United Church of Christ in the USA was a major supporter of the Council. We had to raise funds from the outside for all the work of the Council because the churches in British Honduras did not have sufficient funds and neither did the government. I had met Al Bartholomew at an ecumenical meeting in the United States. I had invited him and others that I met to come to British Honduras to visit. He was in charge of United Church of Christ Missions in Central America, so he stopped here several times on his way to their Missions. He was very concerned about the plight of the poor in British Honduras and facilitated United Church of Christ funding for the work of the Council.

Canning and Sewing Projects

One very successful Council project was Pioneer Foods, a women's group concerned with preserving foods. They started a canning project with whatever jars they had available. In 1972 five Friends from the United States visited for several months, Fred Reeve and his wife, Carolyn Mills and her husband, and Thelma Hinslaw. Fred Reeve was an executive with Ball Corporation, a US company that made canning supplies. He donated all the jars and other equipment for canning, so we had the first food preservation project in British Honduras. And it was a great success!

People really bought those jars and were proud that it had been done right here. In order to get everything duty-free, we put government people on the committee. They wanted us to also train women from their groups. They paid all the costs for the women to come in from

CHAPTER SIX: Belize

the rural areas, transportation and subsistence. The government let us use a nice, long building. It was a very appropriate place. I left to go to Earlham School of Religion in 1974 and while I was gone the government took it over. Marie Sharp bought it from the government. Her hot sauce and preserves are still popular in Belize and with tourists.

After I got back we concentrated on the sewing. Every year we had this thing called "Christmas Village". And we had everything to sell for Christmas. We took orders and made all the curtains and clothes for people. We had a little shop where we sold them. We had big boxes packed up to deliver to the owners

One morning someone going to work noticed our shop door was open and called me. I went there and

Sadie Vernon in her Council of Churches office in 1993.
(*Photo by Judy Lumb*)

saw it had all been stolen, $8,000 worth. Someone saw a child with a piece of cloth she recognized because that cloth was not available in British Honduras. She asked the child about it and that is how they were able to cover it up. That child went home and told that she had been asked. There was nothing to do. The shop had a little money, so we just had to pay back the people. We never did recover from that.

Friends Support the Work of the Council

A visit of five Friends was the beginning of Friends' support of projects in British Honduras. The first project was aimed at serving all groups and social classes, especially the 900 families who were then coming to the Council for help. These families were disadvantaged economically and educationally. The crushing circumstances in which they were forced to live had held back their emotional and spiritual development.

Those who came to the Council for help found a positive and progressive outlook. We made every effort to discover and develop their potential. We saw the need for a change of attitude in male-female relationships to allow an appreciation of the developing self.

Services offered were nutrition classes, baby and child care, money management, sewing classes for those who need special motivation, advisory services, sex education.

We developed an apprentice program for school dropouts with George Gabb, who was one of the best sculptors in British Honduras. Ten or fifteen unemployed youth were hanging around his shop doing small jobs. George Gabb was concerned with the situation of the youth. They talked openly with him and he was a good influence in their lives. The Council provided some slight improvement and expansion of his shop, along with additional equipment, which allowed him to teach sculpturing and woodwork to the boys. A reserve fund was set up to pay the boys for their first pieces to give them encouragement.

The total cost of this first project, including new staff, equipment and operating expenses was $4,100 for the first six months. Those were exciting times because we could see lots of new things happening in British Honduras. Friends can be very proud of their contribution to the development of Belize. They came in when there were great needs and the government was unable to meet them. Friends still support projects in Belize today.

Word from Belize

Sadie Vernon was in our office recently and updated us on the work in Belize. ... On a brief roster of programs were listed the ten projects for which Sadie is currently responsible. Included were such things as managing two preschools (each with 100 children and five teachers), a day care center and a hot lunch program, supervising welfare services and clothing distribution; counselling parents and pregnant teenagers; and overseeing the project that aids Salvadoran refugees in migrating to Canada.

Sadie is an advisor and fund-raiser for the Belize Continuation School where 102 girls from low-income families study home economics, practical arts, beauty culture and business education. The majority of Continuation School graduates are able to find employment after graduation. The Human Development Center, for which Sadie is an advisor, is a skills training and outlet store ... The adult literacy program is rapidly expanding Trayce Peterson, an FUM volunteer, along with a Catholic nun, teaches literacy classes either at the Friends Center or at a school in a surrounding town to classes of about 10 adults who meet over a weekend for the intensive training courses.

The project Sadie seemed most excited about was Belwood Industries, a woman's woodworking shop and five women have been trained in the use and operation of the tools and equipment. The women make puzzles, little toys, games, blackboard desks, children's rockers and benches, which are sold to schools and the public.

Sadie anticipates that with more training on the lathe and additional business management knowledge, this project can turn more profit for their labours.

But as Sadie was leaving, she smiled and said, "It would be easy to get depressed about Belize, but too many good things are happening!" Please remember Sadie, Trayce and the people of Belize in your prayers.

(*Quaker Life* December 1984)

Belize Council of Churches

When I left my job to go to attend the Earlham School of Religion in 1974, I expected to be on leave without pay. I knew it would neither give me prestige, a better job, nor more pay. I just wanted to be better prepared for the work I was doing. I did not want to return to the responsibilities of the desk and consulted with the Executive Committee of the Christian Social Council about having me serve as a Coordinator on my return. I would do the programmes like training of women, work with the Parent Teacher Associations of schools and coordinator of work at the Belize Continuation School. There would be two Departments, Missions, relating to inter-church matters, and Service, relating to social services, training and development. I would do the Service area.

I really expected to find this in place, but I returned to find none of it had even been discussed. Several of the people with whom I had spoken had left the country, so I really had no job. The Council had hired Harvey Jeffreys to be the Executive Secretary and he was going a fine job with the administrative work, but there was nothing in the budget for the Coordinator position.

I did not make any fuss. I could have gone back to the United States, but I did not want to do that. From the beginning I had raised funds to keep the Council going. I liked the job and I wanted to keep it. At every ecumenical meeting we would talk about what we were

Chapter Six: Belize

doing and others got interested. I invited people from all different churches to visit British Honduras.

Church Women United in the US had promised to send me some money, so I was able to stay on and work with women. The local Church Women United had raised the money to extend the Christian Social Council building on Allenby to twice its size. So, the Council was on one side and I worked with women on the other side. It was what I wanted anyway because I did not care about the desk work, I cared about the people work.

Harvey Jeffreys was first class. He did an excellent job with the preschools and the other projects of the council. But he only stayed one year more after I returned. After he left we reorganized. The Executive Committee of the Christian Council was responsible for general oversight and each project had a committee that handled the daily work—the Mina Grant Day Care Centre, the Yarlborough Preschool, the Pine Street Preschool, and the Continuation School. I resumed the Executive Secretary position, but the desk work was minimized, which allowed me to concentrate on the people work.

The Council's name evolved from Christian Social Council to Belize Christian Council and, finally to the Belize Council of Churches in 1985. From the formation of the Council in 1957 until 1984 we had good support from external sources and were able to do many things. But it was in 1984 when I realized we did not have the financial backing we used to have. All the funding agencies found their money had tightened up, so they had to tighten up on us. Another factor in the financial crisis was competition. Young professional social workers realized that money was available for these kinds of projects. We had known that for a long time and for years we were the only ones getting it. When new non-governmental organizations (NGOs) were formed in the early 1980s, they competed with us for the limited funds available.

We wanted to keep doing the same things, but we had to find other ways of achieving our objectives. This is where the program began to take a turn toward a period of containment and it continued in a gradual decline to the present time. If we had not gotten support for the Continuation School from the government, we would have had to shut it down.

I continued in my position as Executive Secretary of the Council until my retirement in 1997. Over the 35 years I worked for the Council, the scope of work was very broad and allowed me to be deeply involved in social services for the people of Belize. It provided me a good vehicle for the kind of work I wanted to do. Along with my executive duties, I was given the freedom to serve the community in these many ways. Some of these things would never have happened if I had to go to a meeting and present a complete plan to get permission. But nobody ever asked me to do that. I had the freedom to move. And it did not mean I was at a desk as an Executive Secretary all the time. The desk work was very little. Growing up with an agency has its advantages but also its disadvantages. My work with the Council was a unique type of service that was demanding but intensely surprising and rewarding.

State of the Nation

This is only one example of many, many speeches I have given in Belize. The Lions asked me to speak about ten years ago. A politician reminded me of it much later, saying,

"I cannot get away from you. I can almost hear what you said to the Lions about social fracture and what would happen if we did not do anything about it. Before that speech, I had never heard about that at all. But I see it now. We are now faced with violent social fracture just as you predicted."

After Hurricane Hattie was the beginning of social fracture in British Honduras, when parents began leaving their children with grandparents. Because we had no houses for people to live in, free plane rides to

CHAPTER SIX: Belize

the States were offered to people who had somebody there to sponsor them. That was when the migration to the States began. And nothing was done to correct it.

Here is an excerpt from that speech to the Lion's Club:

The state of the union—who is responsible? The government, parents, the public in general, churches, school?

It's no use talking about how it was years ago, and yet memories die hard, like the broken bread cart stopping by your house and those bread with two ends that could hold condensed milk—yum yum! Ah Mr. Pittison, you were such good fun for us children. I was sorry when you gave up delivering bread. In those days you were selling for someone else, Mr. Lyon, but now, Mr. Sonny, your son, has his own bakery. I love it!

Old people used to care about children, but then children were taught to care about old people, too. This was not done by the lecture system, but by love in action. You were often sent to take some goodies to them. I well remember Mother Jenkins. On Sundays after church, my brother and I had to see Miss Adel and Miss Amy, and to visit Miss Mary with that terribly ulcerated leg! Miss Mary was always in pain and, believe me, for one as sensitive as I was to such things, my solar plexus got very busy. But Miss Mary had lots of fruit trees, so she would send us to see if there were plums, pomegranates, guavas, jumbilin, or mangos that might have dropped from the neighbour's tree.

One Sunday in church I felt like running up to the minister and putting my finger in his face because he was telling us about "God is Love" and how God cares for all of us. I could not see it at all. For myself, yes, but for those I visited on Sundays, NO, NO, NO! But those were child thoughts and I am glad that I learned to care about the old. It distresses me to see and hear how many young treat the old today.

There is a Jamaican proverb that says, "Man wey no done grow mustn't laugh after long man" Good advice indeed!

Here is a story to help you see why I am troubled. An old man who had a broken leg was able to push his fruit and vegetable cart around. He pushed his cart all over town and always talked as if he was in pain.

Some youths, caught in the saying that Satan finds some mischief for idle hands, got what to them was a great idea of a practical joke. They put a stick between the spokes so that when the man pushed the cart after completing a sale, something would happen.

It did, and the whole cart toppled over, scattering the old man's wares. They laughed and laughed while adults around helped the old man put his things together. They disappeared. Now that was twelve years ago.

Social fracture began happening right after Hurricane Hattie. Now we are faced with violent social fracture. Who is responsible? We all are. The society cared about its children and youth and they, though sometimes upset with the old, had to show respect. So the second priority of caring for others gets fouled up.

One of the serious difficulties of our time is in the third ordering of life, which allows us to realize that the first two are instructions for life and they are orders. But who wants to take orders?

We are well aware that we are set in families where this most important learning should begin, where children learn to feel the good, the givingness of God and the ordered life.

Modern man feels he has found a better way. Parental responsibility has so often denied the young this essential experience. Jesus went to Nazareth and was subject to his parents.

Jesus has touched the nation at every point—economics, politics, culture, religion, rich, poor, citizen, alien, friend, foe, old, young, male, female, godly, ungodly—all sorts and conditions. Now he is at the centre of things, the sphere of influence, and found it wanting. He could do nothing about the attitudes but he

CHAPTER SIX: *Belize* 167

could attempt an ordering and, in a final act of authority he removes the trespassers. That done, he takes up the work not yet completed. He still has hope and he goes on teaching daily in the temple.

Chapter Seven
Space, Time and Eternity

My latest thought is that at the time of ongoing, my spirit will be taken from the body by a messenger of God. Because I know that I came from God, I must keep the faith that I will some day return to God.

Feelings I Do Not Understand

Jesus tried to teach us, "You are the light, you are the net," and so on. I am aware of being different from the information I get through my five senses. I have a very strong feeling, sensing nature. But over and beyond that, I am deeply intuitive moving into an area that goes into predictions, particularly about deaths and accidents. I always knew, even as a small child, that I was different from other children. If I talked about some of the things I saw or experienced, they would think I was crazy. I think I have experienced things that most people do not.

Sometimes, in my efforts to make sure that God knows what he has been about in my life, I go into a question and answer thing. And God, instead of explaining or giving me something to meet my need to know what or why, has always some up with, "I hear you. I know." That is all I ever get. Some things I have left alone and have stopped asking for explanations.

CHAPTER SEVEN: Space, Time and Eternity 169

I keep going back to when I was four years old. I can see my little body lying there in Ga's double bed. I always put my head to the foot of the bed. As I was waking up, I felt that I was "big", that somehow I had the body of an adult, though I was conscious of being a child. I felt I was brought back by a spirit being who placed me in my body after which I woke up.

Sometimes Ga would try to wake me up, and I could not be awakened. After a while I could wake up, but I would have a dull headache all day. Finally, my aunt with whom I slept knew something was going on that she did not understand, so she told the others not to wake me up, but to let me wake up by myself. It was not every day, but it was quite often. It went on until I was seven and then no more.

I never told anyone about it, not even my grandmother. It still troubles me. I still want to know where I went, why I went, who took me and brought me back. I saw the return but not the going. This remains a troubling enigma. I have read many books and articles hoping for a clue, but all in vain.

In later years as I have come to know God as very purposeful, I have tried to get an explanation. I have pleaded the case saying I was but a child, that I needed to know where I went, why I went, and who was involved in the taking and the returning. I have been able to talk with people about it for a few years now. None of them has ever heard of such a thing, and none had any suggestions about it. It may well have to do with what my grandmother said was second sight. My latest thought is that at the time of ongoing, my spirit will be taken from the body by a messenger of God. Because I know that I came from God. I must keep the faith that I will some day return to God.

One morning I woke up very sad and my grandmother finally got me to tell her what my tears were about. I had a dream in which I saw my dear Uncle Perry in a coffin in the parlour. She assured me that he was well, that she had heard from him and he would be home soon. I felt better but so needed to see him. In a few weeks he came and I felt better. Then it happened. A few weeks later he felt ill and never recovered. There he was in that coffin, just as I had seen him. It was a devastating to a five-year old. My grandmother took me aside for she knew I wanted an explanation

"You have second sight. If you see anything like this again, don't tell everybody. Just tell me. People will want to pay you to tell them what you see. Do not ever get that started."

I did not want to see anything like that again. As a child I seemed free of it. But after leaving home I was made aware before a member of my family passed on, particularly members of my mother's family. At my grandmother's passing I was in "cobwebs" for a whole day and that night I dreamed of angels carrying her away. My Uncle Wallace, or Pardy, as he was called by the nephews and nieces, died when I was away, too. His death was also made known as I saw angels come into the room and carry him away.

For Ga, my aunt who really reared me, it was different. I was travelling and there were cobwebs all day. I got back to the hotel in Cleveland quite late. I was tired and uneasy and hardly slept, but early the next morning I fell into a deep sleep. I dreamt that I was in British Honduras, walking to church. As I passed the green there was a coffin standing up with someone in it. I made out the body of my aunt but could not see her face. It was Ascension Day and I knew she always went to early church on that day. Later I heard that she took ill on Ascension Day.

When I returned to Indiana late on Saturday I called my Aunt Agnes to tell her of my dream. She had married an American man and was living in Indianapolis. She was anxious as I was and told me her dream,

CHAPTER SEVEN: Space, Time and Eternity 171

I heard someone at the door and when I went, there were two aunts long dead on each side of my sister, holding her. They all wore black skirts and white blouses. I was very glad to see them and invited them in; then I went to the kitchen for fix some refreshments for them. When I came out with the tray, they had all gone.

She and I knew what we would hear. As we were talking, she said she hoped they would let us know what was going on. As I put the phone down, there was an incoming call from Western Union. Ga had passed away that morning and the funeral would be the next day. It was a hard blow because I was hoping to return at the end of September so I could give her some care. She knew that.

Ga was very strict and she really used up her energies trying to straighten out the world. She taught a number of people who were very successful in life because she gave them good basic skills on which they could build. Many children who seemed unable to learn elsewhere were brought to her school and most of them were able to get straightened out and be successful. She had been organist at the Cathedral for 50 years and had been honoured by Her Majesty Queen Elizabeth II and made a Member of the British Empire.

Visions

One day a friend who lives in the United States asked something of me. First of all, she wanted to know if I had made a will. I asked her what she thought I would have to make a will for and who would benefit. We talked for awhile. Then she interrupted,

"Let me ask you a favour. I would like to have your papers, every paper found with your writing on it. Just ask someone in your family to put all your papers in a box and send them to me. I am even willing to fly to Belize to collect them."

She already has her own collection for every time we are together she tried to write something down. She always has a string of questions and the last time we were together she said,

"I notice that you never change the answers to any of the questions. Why is that?"

Life gave me many certainties along the way, and though there has been an expanding of some consciousness, some basic truths remain. I began in a family and learned about life there, but home, school, and church never had answers to satisfy me. In fact, I soon realized that the kinds of questions I had were too far out anyway.

Sometimes I asked my grandmother a few things. She gave me an important direction true until now. "If you want to know something very badly, keep your mouth shut and your ears open. That way you'll get the truth. Otherwise people will lie to you about what they don't know and you will get into a lot of trouble. Be a good listener, child, and see how much you will find out about what you must know."

Time and again I have seen this to be true. I may need information badly but I do not know who would have it. Sometimes I think of persons who should have it, but have no leading to ask this one or that one. Sometimes a person comes to see me and as we talk about things the information I was seeking is there.

Many people who do get the information do not even acknowledge the fact that often outside of their own doing, they come to it and hit upon the thing or the answers they sought. By a brilliant flash of light, of insight, discover something new to the world, but old to life itself.

It is really amazing how life has directions that cannot be manipulated at will. It already has all the answers and as these move in an "everywhere, every moment" fashion, it drops the information where and when it finds the slots ready to receive it. If "there is no new thing under the sun" (*Ecclesiastes* 1:9), then

CHAPTER SEVEN: Space, Time and Eternity   173

why do we not make ourselves available to the most learnings we could have?

Some experiences are extrasensory, outside the usual five senses. Sight and hearing are two of our most fascinating senses. Their extensions into the ether all around us are sometimes frightening because they are out of the ordinary, but they are also exciting and real.

The bulk of humanity exists in community consciousness. The place where they live is their everyday lives. Some venture into what has been called "horizon consciousness." Seeing is believing. The ships that come into the horizon may have come from far away places. Many of us can look at thought and ideas, and we see where are they coming from—the surrounding sea—for "there is no new thing under the sun."

One day when I was in the U.S., in fact, it was May 11, 1962, at 2 p.m. and I was reading the sixth chapter of the Gospel of John. Marcus Kendall had gone to work and his wife Evelyn was at the beauty shop. I sat by a window on that beautiful afternoon. I was aware of a being outside the window. A male figure dressed in a soldier's uniform—all in white—was kneeling on one knee with a sword in a sheath in his right hand.

There was no movement, no voice, and after a brief time, the vision faded. I have not understood it clearly, but I believe God has assigned me a defender. I still hope to understand it more clearly some day.

I often have these visions. It is commonplace to have a vision of a man dressed in white. I think it is one of Michael's group of angels that is my guardian angel. Whenever I get this vision, I know something good is going to happen.

My mother appeared in my dreams for a long time. It only stopped a few years ago. I think it means she has moved on to some other place. When she would appear, it was usually a warning that something bad was going to happen. But with her watching over me, I knew I was going to come out all right.

The most dramatic was when she told me on South Caicos Island to put all of my clothes and things up and to take that money with me that was not mine. I was staying at the Commissioner's house then. It was up a little hill. The police came to take us away because a hurricane was coming. I put all of my things my clothes and everything, on the bed and rolled the mattress over them. After the hurricane, when we went back, my room was the only dry one. The family's children had the measles so they had my dry bed to lie in.

Recently I was bothered by a spirit that I did not think came from God. Each night as I knelt down to pray, I would feel these hands on my shoulders holding me back. One day I saw a person. All I could see was a brown skirt and brown shoes, so I knew it was a female. All my other visions had always been males dressed in white. I was sure this was an evil spirit, so I called Rev. Erskine of the Church of God. He and his wife are well known for getting rid of undesirable spirits. And lots of people are having these kinds of problems. Sometimes they are spirits of ancestors. A friend was having similar problem. Just as she was about to go to sleep, she was bothered by spirits. Her son was bothered also. I told her to see Rev. Erskine. He told her she should be baptized and she agreed. Afterwards she told me that she had only peaceful sleep, no more spirits.

Rev. Erskine said to me, "I know about your beliefs, but I tell you this has helped other people. I think you should be baptized."

So, early one Sunday morning we went down to the sea by the Fisheries Wharf and I was baptized. I have not been bothered since.

My body gets tired often but my mind is very active and that is a wonderful gift from God. I would like to have a steady income and just to live a kind, caring, witnessing life. For God is love and I love my God and my Saviour Jesus Christ, and have been so blessed by the Spirit.

When it is time to finish, one should go and trust in the Lord. I am very uncertain about the future. It is the first time I have not have pointers. This time I am not certain what to do next. There are a lot of things I want to do, but I have no clear direction.

Communication with the Dead

My understanding of death or transition and also of vibrations does not allow me to appreciate communication with the dead. It is possible, but when one considers that our state of spiritual preparedness determines our progression in the next life, all I believe is that those who have passed over and can be contacted so easily have remained earthbound. Their spiritual energies were insufficient to refine them enough to reach the higher planes of existence. Instead of the yearning and longing for the mansion prepared by Christ, they were forgetful that "he that loveth father or mother more than me is not worthy of me." They were family-oriented instead of Christ-oriented. Surely they know and they see and they hear, but to depend on that is to exchange our birthright for a mess of pottage.

Yes, the next stage for such is almost like this one, only the vibrations are faster and beyond normal sight and hearing. Those gifted with the ability can hear these higher tones and see also.

A friend of mine told me she "saw" her father and asked him if he "saw" her mother. He told her he saw her. He knew where she was, but he could not contact her! The father was a Jew and did not believe in Christ. The mother was a Christian. I am reminded of Dives and Lazaras—the same thing. They were separated by a great gulf. Dives was prepared for one range and Lazarus for another.

I do not say that at times our loved ones, or other spirits may not be allowed to reach us for very special reasons. I believe that, just as Gabriel appeared to Mary, or other spiritual beings have appeared as we read in the Bible. That I fully understand now.

So, this is why I am not for this business of communicating with the dead. I have a book here on communication, but for me it has no interest. I can see how some people would go for it and how it may help. But as a believer in Christ, I feel that the people who want and need communication are selling their faith in Christ a little short. Further, they are binding themselves with chains that will be hard to break. I believe that if someone starts that kind of thing and gets in touch with a loved one who is dead one time, they well want to keep doing it. So, it becomes a danger.

I hope that when I go, I can make it to that place promised by Christ. I am trying to orient my mind and spirit, my conscious and subconscious towards Him and, though the progression is far from perfect, I am trying and feel sure that Christ will take care of things as I have faith to believe.

Of course, I hope I can live to see the day when spiritual energies will be enough to transform the body so that we will not die as man now dies, but that is a long hard pull.

Tune up your spirit, work at communication with God's Holy Spirit, try to find those important few moments for meditation and sooner or later you will know and see and hear those things which God has prepared for you from the foundation of the world.

Living and Working Alone

People in the United States ask me how I manage without the support of a Friends community. Friends do not see how I can be here alone. But I do not need that. Quakerism prepares you for the aloneness. That is the essence of it—you and God, God in Jesus Christ and the Holy Spirit—that is the cell theory. It is only the outward expression of the faith for me to be with you who believe the same as I do, but that has nothing to do with me. I am my own little cell here with the Quaker thing and then I reach out to any brothers and sisters who believe the same as I do.

CHAPTER SEVEN: Space, Time and Eternity

When I go to the United States, I go to the lonely places because that is where I thrive. That is where I get growth and development because then I am reaching out to all of life for the sustenance. I am not depending on others and going to meetings. That is not where it is at for me. The whole world is here and I am in the middle of all that is around me.

Belizeans do not understand this either. They do not believe that anyone can live like I do and not be lonely. They ask me how I could live in South Caicos Island for five years, but they were five happy years! Sometimes there was a water shortage, sometimes food shortage. Everybody is different. I am well satisfied with the way I live. If you do not have the internal mechanism to handle it, you had better not try it. That is not given to me by anyone but God. God knows the lonely places where I have survived and thrived.

I do not feel like I have to have people around all the time. In fact, if I had it here, I would run away from it. I could not exist with a crowd around me all the time. I do not have to feel out and see if my friend Mary is there. If she comes, I am glad to see her.

I never feel lonely. Lonely for what? I can read. I can think. I lay down in my bed at night and thank God for giving me good eyesight. I can read even the finest print without any eyeglasses. I read and think what it means, and how I fit into that. I do not need to talk to people all the time. It is from within myself that everything arises.

Living Without Fear

I really do not have any fear. I do not know anything I am afraid of. Fear is just not a part of my make-up. When I heard something outside, I would get up to open the door. My family could not tolerate that. They would say, "Why you open the door? You don't know who is outside."

But I would open the door to see what's there, whether there is anything to be concerned about.

I do not talk about being afraid. I hate to feel afraid of anything. I do not like that feeling, so I avoid it, especially if I have concern for a situation.

That carries over into my desire to learn about religions and spirituality. I read a wide variety of literature. I am not afraid to be influenced by anything. I pick what I want and leave the rest.

But sometimes I go back later because I come to understand what was being said. At the time I had folded it up, but rather than write it off as nonsense, I just put it away. Then when I am better able to understand and use it, I go back. I might be reading something else and remember where I read that thing. Then I understand it and accept it most of the time. Some people think this is absolute nonsense, but to me it is not, it is a marvelous thing.

An example is my recent experience with the Moonies. I listened to the Moonie women when other people were afraid that it would rub off on me. But I am never afraid that it would rub off on me. I am going to look at it because I am secure with what I know and what I believe. I am not searching for something to believe. I already know. So I could listen to the Moonies and sympathize with them for what the public was doing to them because I did not feel the same way.

The Moonies came to my office nearly every day, some of them, because they wanted somebody who had accepted them. They were dealing with nonacceptance a lot of the way. I did not understand the whole thing, but I accepted them as persons who came here to do what they thought was a very important task for them.

But they were rejected without being even considered. That bothered me, so I said to my friend in immigration, "You did not even listen to what the people were saying. You just heard they were Moonies and wrote them off. That's no way to deal with people who come into this society. Why did not you accept the Moonies?"

CHAPTER SEVEN: Space, Time and Eternity 179

He said, "Who accepts them?"

I said, "I do," and he burst out laughing.

In each of us there is some bad and some good. We will find what we are looking for. And I know that those people brought a lot of love, a lot of caring. The immigration man is supposed to come and see my birthday poster that they made. I've never had a poster like that. And it was not a bought one. Within their philosophy they made things rather than buying them, even a card. They use old cards and fix up a new one. Make something new out of the old. And the card they brought me is one they designed and made because they thought it was something I would appreciate. And it is—it is a nice big thing that says, "Happy Birthday!" The Moonies were thinking of my birthday and nobody else was. A lot of other people knew my birthday, but the Moonies brought the card and they were so happy doing it. It just gave me an idea about them just as everybody else was condemning them. The upper level people were condemning them as Moonies, but they forgot the human element even in Moonies. I do not like to write off anybody.

I bet you that these Moonies women visited more Belizeans than any other organization that has been here. They went around visiting people and they were in every district for some three months. The immigration people did not know that they were in the districts and nobody bothered them.

I think that they had some good to offer us, but anyway that is beside the point now. They had to go and went with bitter tears because they made some very good friends. I was invited to their farewell dinner and the ladies cried and cried. They invited Belizeans to share their farewell because the government refused to accept them.

In the morning before they left, six of the ladies were at my office and wanted to talk. They just needed someone to listen and to hear how they were feeling and how disappointed they were because of all the things they could do. So I promised them that even though the government may not let them return, I would still talk to the immigration men about their attitudes and religious defence of Christianity. I may defend Christianity, but I am not going to be foolish about it. Some Christians feel that Christianity has to be thus and so, and no other way. But they need to understand what Christianity is all about.

Obscenities

Now and then I get a pleasant surprise when someone, realizing that they have given me an earful, asks to be excused. I have told myself that some day I will make an attempt to start a conversation about obscenities.

Obscenities undermine our personhood. And I believe they are giving us messages about society that we would do well to heed. I believe that we are a society under stress, all sorts of stresses—economical, societal, psychological, political—all playing their part in keeping us wondering what is next. How much more will the cost of living go up? There is Guatemala with that old drum beat in our ears.

Sometimes it seems that permissiveness has become an ideal, or that free speech gives the freedom to be obscene and abusive. It could also be part of the identity crisis we are undergoing.

Then I think of the Church and wonder about its mission and where it really is in all of this confusion of thought and life. I read and reread relevant parts of the Scriptures. I revise my learnings about behaviours and can hear people like Marshall McLuhan and Eric Hoffer and Hans Selye. They tried to explain these behaviours.

I also try the deeply religious ones and hear Eric Routley saying he is writing for an unbiblical generation, as he attempts to bring relevance to the Old Testament, and he does it well. After waxing through a book called

CHAPTER SEVEN: Space, Time and Eternity

Down Peacock's Feathers, I am convinced that there is serious need for self-examination and admission of wrongdoing and repentance.

These behaviours will pass; for surely there will be a time when people will have no need to identify themselves or receive attention through the use of obscenities and abuse, through destructiveness and disrespect of self.

I realize that the adults of my early years were busy trying to prepare my generation for a certain kind of life, and that church, school, family and society were deeply involved. There is no denying their protectiveness, but at the same time they saw to it that we were exposed to sickness, pain and need, for we were their messengers sent to find out about the sick or to take goodies to the house-bound and to the needy. Few were well off, but sharing was a part of living and they gave, not of abundance, but out of their sense of being blessed.

The church provided some social activities and education services as well as opportunities for organizational development. It cared whether I was there on Sundays, for if I missed Church or Sunday School someone wanted to know what had happened to me.

This upward move is one deeply recognized by Christians and especially so in the Eucharistic churches—in the Anglican Communion. Listen to it closely:

Priest—Lift up your hearts.

Response—We lift them up unto the Lord.

A serious act affirming the upward movement of God affirms the rule of God in our lives. This lifting up to which we are called is significant. The *sursum corda* as we know it is, or should be, a high moment of answering to God's call to help the whole world into the faith in that God who urges us to make an answer. Always a great response happens to us and in that moment, we are lifted up, not only for ourselves, but to commit ourselves in heart and mind, and in deed and word, to the work of God. The upward lift is both irresistible and inevitable to believers.

Now we know that we members of the Church have a proclamation to make. This life work of the Church must proclaim the Cross. Christ was crucified for the sin of the world. With the saving power of Christ we are ready for missions.

The greatest reserve force in Christendom is that to be found in the thousands who make up the church. Lay evangelism is vital to its life and growth, but we must also experience in ourselves the need for Lent experiences in the collective. There is always the need for a new and contrite heart.

And I realize that I have not gotten away from all that liturgy. And though I am Quaker now and we do not go into all that, but within myself there is a part that will never leave me—never, ever. I have my moments when I sit down and be a good Quaker and read something. But there are many, many times when it's the ongoingness of things and then I hear the songs that I know by heart. Every year they were repeated—fifteen, sixteen, seventeen years—and I knew them all. I chant them and they come like second nature to me. In difficult circumstances I call on those things.

One day I said, "Lord, look here now. You know I read about David and I read how David asked you to 'make haste, Oh Lord, to help me.'"

He had a problem. But those were the terms he used to talk to God, because he was in a constant conversation with God, and he related almost every aspect of life to this God, Creator. Well, he never had Jesus Christ, but it was God.

I said, "Lord, I have to come to you, just like David came. And I feel You are supposed to hear me the same way. Yes, I am in a situation and you are the only one I

CHAPTER SEVEN: Space, Time and Eternity 183

can look to. So, I am looking now to see how you make haste to help me, how you are going to answer that."

And the next day, the thing I needed was already in the Post Office, but the day when I needed it so badly I did not have it in my hand. So, I said, "Praise God, make haste to help me."

The next night I said, "Lord, you already knew it was coming to trouble and you had already done something for it. Now I have to know another way of trusting that verse, "Before you call I will answer, and while you are yet speaking, I will hear.'"

Space, Time and Eternity

When I was growing up, books were not so common. We had a few magazines. I was never interested in *True Story* and those kinds of magazines, but there were others having to do with clothing or food that interested me. Aunt Nora used to bring home all the magazines they threw out at the Priest's Office where she worked.

I was able to read at night when I was supposed to be asleep. The light came in the window from the street lamp right onto my book. I pushed whatever I was reading down by the bed and my aunt never found it. You have to find ways to achieve your goal. That light shining in my window was a life-saver for me. I really did a lot of reading.

Back in 1934 I went to visit my only paternal aunt, Aunt Agatha, who was a suffering giant. She was married to a highly intelligent man whose possibilities were tremendous but he was living in the shadow of alcohol. His creative energies were terribly misused. I knew he was searching because one day I found the trash box filled with papers and booklets he had thrown away.

My aunt asked me what I was going to do with all that rubbish.

"Read," I told her, and that I did.

I picked out some, took them home and hid them away to read. Though they were religious, I knew they would have been taken away and I would have been severely reprimanded for reading such matters.

I read all the Rosicrucian things and threw them away. Then I read all the Unity things and hid them because I read the famous Unity prayer, "God is my help in every need." I wanted to learn it. It felt true and gave me a concept of God that added to what I already knew. I did not understand it fully, but I learned it and put it in reserve. I read the copies of *Daily Word* over and over and the *Unity Magazines* were heavier reading but there were some good stories and poems.

A part of me was responding even though perceptions of the truth being presented were clouded. Unfolding were such good ideas and levels of consciousness that urged interior development. My heart was ready to be touched by this new teaching and I know it was this readiness that led me there on that particular day. I still read *Daily Word* and *Unity Magazine* and I send in prayers for others as well as myself.

I am not afraid. I am secure in my faith. I can explore other things and take what I want but leave the rest. Sometimes I read something and do not understand it at the time. Later it will come to me and I will go back to it and then I see what it means.

I really am sorry that when I was young I did not have anybody to put me into science, because that really is where I am. People ask what magazines I want and are always surprised when I say *Omni* and *Discover*. They do not look at me as someone who is into all that science. But it explains life to me and especially the invisible.

The invisible is a marvelous thing, the way God made it so you could see it, but it is really nothing at all. It is only there for us to learn what we must learn. We understand how we are made of atoms and they are all alike and they are all changing by the minute. These are all the wonders

CHAPTER SEVEN: Space, Time and Eternity 185

of God. And it could not happen without Light. Let there be Light! That is why Light had to be the first thing because all the rest is based on Light. I have my finest moments at night when I read and get into these things.

I have had to deal with second sight for that remains an important part of my dilemma. Feelings also have to be reckoned with since there were feelings before seeing and hearing. When I read Dr. Stromberg where he wrote of a fifth dimension, ESP and telepathy, it became clearer to me, though they were already valid for me. I have to live in a finite world, but Stromberg's article in the 1961 *Journal of the Franklin Institute* entitled "Space, Time and Eternity" cleared up a lot of the mysteries. The greatest thing about this man's thinking remains this: All knowledge given to him was for the good of all and his final paper is for all to read, write about, and quote. It was published with no copyright. What a great gift that was for those of us who need this kind of help on our journey into Light! Quakerism encouraged me to be unafraid of the mind and my own place in the Universe, as well as to move into Truth as it is revealed to me as I enjoy this multidimensional world.

Long ago I read an article dealing with our sense of time and *Ecclesiastics* 1:9, "There is no new thing under the sun." The article said that we live in the slowest time zone and what happens here as we see it, has already happened in another time, so it is possible to see and experience fully something that has not yet reached us or happened in this slowest of time zones. It may be true that we function in a very slow time zone, and there are multi-levels of activity. Time on television is speeded up so that we see whole events in half an hour, events that would take much longer in real life. In a way it explains second sight, which should really be called first sight.

Most of my sightings have had to do with death or with accidents and in only one instance has the time span between the knowing and the event been longer than six weeks. I am still trying to get God to explain my experiences between the ages of four and seven. I still feel I am entitled to an answer.

If may well be that when the time comes for the final separation of spirit from body, I will just go to sleep and will not know who will take the spirit away or where I will be taken, but there will be no return. As a Christian and a believer in a purposeful God, I hope I will have a consciousness of going and will hear God say, "You can come to stay now and be right here with me forever."

Appendix: Honours and Awards

The following is a partial list of the honours and awards that Sadie Vernon has received.

Outstanding Citizen Award, St. John's College
October 31, 1971

Personality of the Month, *The New Belize*
January, 1983

Sadie Vernon—An Advocate for the Voiceless and Powerless

She seems always so very busy. Her phones keep ringing; she had one meeting and another, then an appointment to meet with visiting officials of Crossroads International. This is a voluntary service organization of which she is the local representative.

But our study of Sadie Vernon started even before she agreed to keep the appointment with us. While waiting in her office on Allenby Street in Belize City, which is the headquarters of the Belize Christian Council, we made some mental notes of what we saw and heard.

Miss Vernon is a highly respected woman in the community and she is very much liked by her staff of full-time and voluntary workers.

Born in Belize City, as a young girl she attended St. Hilda's College. After graduating she went to Jamaica where she taught for a number of years in primary and secondary schools. She also taught in the Turks and Caicos Islands. She later studied nursing in the United States of America and graduated from the Indianapolis School of Practical Nursing in 1957.

She studied social work at the Centre of Continuing Studies in Chicago after which she worked for awhile with the Greater Church Federation of Chicago.

Miss Vernon returned home in 1960 when she took up an appointment with the YWCA. But in 1961 she went back to the United States. However, her talents were needed at home and she was offered a job as the Executive Secretary of the Christian Social Council, which is now the Belize Christian Council.

However, during her twenty years of service with this organization Miss Vernon again did a stint in the United States studying for the ministry. She is "convinced Quaker" and holds a Master of Ministry degree from the Earlham School of Religion, a Quaker Seminary in Richmond, Indiana.

This outstanding Belizean woman has committed her life to working with the less privileged. She believes that there must be an advocate for the voiceless and powerless and her energies are directed towards the uplifting of the less privileged class in our society.

In her work she is involved in a number of advisory councils including the Legal Aid Council, the Council of Voluntary Social Services, as well as various projects and programmes for human development.

Miss Vernon believes that the Belize Christian Council is playing a very important role in Belizean Society and she would like to see the strengthening of the ecumenical movement in Belize. She is keenly interested in the family and plans to intensify the activities of the Christian Council towards more family life activities.

"Many more women need to develop greater awareness in the areas of politics, technology, management, theology, and ministry if women are to take their places in the vanguard of Belizeans who work to enhance the development process," she says.

She is a Sunday School teacher at St. Andrews, the Presbyterian Church in Belize City. Her other interests are music, arts and crafts and stamp collecting.

Sadie Vernon is one who has been chosen in the service of God to live a life of advocacy for those among us who have been battered by the proverbial "slings and arrows of outrageous fortune". She radiates hope!

(*The New Belize*, January 1983)

Outstanding Volunteer of the Year Award, Belize Council of Voluntary Social Services—1986

Commander of the Most Excellent Order of the British Empire—July, 1987

Distinguished Alumnus Earlham School of Religion—1988

Honorary Doctor of Divinity Earlham School of Religion—June 9, 1991

Sadie Vernon, a Belizean Quaker and 1976 graduate of Earlham School of Religion, is dedicated to helping the poor and disadvantaged people of her country. She has worked for nearly thirty years as the Executive Secretary of the Belize Council of Churches, developing and administering programs for families, teenagers, and children.

She was born into an Anglican family in Belize and educated at St. Hilda's College for girls. During World

War II, Sadie visited Jamaica. Realizing she would not be able to return home, she taught in various places in Jamaica and the Bahamas. In 1949, she began teaching at Highgate Continuation School in Jamaica where she became acquainted with Friends.

In 1961, she returned to Belize and was invited to become the first native Executive Secretary of the Christian Social Council, which has since become the Belize Council of Churches. Her work with the Council placed her in the midst of crisis as Belize struggled to cope with the devastating effects of Hurricane Hattie. Sadie organized the distribution of food and clothing in the aftermath of the hurricane.

For the last quarter century, Sadie has occupied a modest office on Allenby Street in Belize City. From her headquarters she has directly touched the lives of thousands of Belizeans of all ages. She has responded to the needs of children in the Council of Churches schools, to young people with personal problems, and she has provided comfort and support to the aging. She has also aided Belizean natives in their effort to market and sell their crafts in ways that are economically equitable.

Friends have been supportive of Sadie's ministries through the Council, particularly the Belize Continuation School, an alternative educational opportunity for teenage girls who are not able to attend regular high school; the hot lunch program for primary school children; the Human Development Center; a skills training outlet store; and the Society of Friends Youth Center (opened in 1982), which houses a small class of remedial students.

In addition to her work at the Council of Churches, Sadie Vernon serves on many committees and boards of directors. She has been called on frequently to speak to groups about Belize and Belizean cultures, a subject close to her heart. In addition, the international community has sought her for advice and insights.

In the early 1970s, Sadie's dream was to attend Earlham School of Religion and broaden both her theological understanding and her skills for practical ministry. In 1976 she was awarded the Master of Ministry of degree. In 1986 the Belize Council of Voluntary Social Services named Sadie the first recipient of the Outstanding Volunteer of the Year Award. A Queen's medal of honour (Commander of the Most Excellent Order of the British Empire—CBE) was bestowed on her in June of 1987. At the 1988 Alumni Gathering of ESR, Sadie was present to receive the ESR Alumni Award in honour of her life and work.

(*Partners in Ministry*, Friends United Meeting)

Sadie Vernon receiving the Honorary Doctor of Divinity in June, 1991. On the left is John Miller, who was acting dean of ESR in 1990-91. On the right is Len Clark, Earlham College Provost. (*Courtesy, Archives of Friends United Meeting*)

Acceptance Speech

It is with a deep sense of gratitude that I accept the Honorary Doctor of Divinity degree from Earlham School of Religion.

It represents a significant honour to my country and people. It presents me with a considerably heightened awareness of who I am, not by virtue of the works, but in the assurance that God is purposeful and manifold gifts were provided for the tasks.

There is also a considerable sense of the unfinished dreams, but I must now continue my journey with greater sense of the Cosmic Vision.

The school was a part of the dream and now I have at last begun to see the unfolding of the dream. The Ministry of Education is ready to help us get the building and we expect that in the near future Phase I building will be started. —Sadie Vernon

Sadie Vernon Receives Honorary Degree

Sadie Vernon received an honorary Doctor of Divinity degree from Earlham College during its June 1991 graduation exercises. This honour was in recognition of her work as a Belizean Quaker helping the poor and disadvantaged people of her country. Sadie has worked for almost thirty years as the Executive Secretary of the Belize Council of Churches, developing and assisting with the programs for families and children. During this time Sadie Vernon has received numerous awards and honours including being named Outstanding Volunteer of the Year in 1986 by the Belize Council of Voluntary Services, a Queen's medal of honour (Commander of the Most Excellent Order of the British Empire—CBE), and the Earlham School of Religion Alumni Award in 1988.

Sadie's work with the people of Belize has been supported through Friends United Meeting since the early 1980s. Through contributions from yearly meetings and from individuals, as well as volunteer services, we continue to support the work of Sadie in Belize. This support has had as its focus the work with teenage girls through the Belize Continuation School, which provides alternative education for teenage girls. Recently, Friends have expanded their efforts in Belize through the beginning of a Friends Meeting in the village of La Democracia.

Friends United Meeting congratulates Sadie on receiving this honour and asks that you join with us a Partners in Ministry in supporting this ministry of love to those in need. (*Partners in Ministry, Friends United Meeting*)

Recorded as a Minister
Western Yearly Meeting
August 3–6, 1994

Paul Harris Award, Rotary International–1997

"It is a pleasure to honour an outstanding Belizean who has lived the Rotary spirit of service above self." These were the words of outgoing President of Rotary Ernesto Vasquez as he presented the highest Rotary award to Sadie Vernon at the Annual Handing Over Ceremony and Awards Night of the Rotary Cllub of Belize held at the Radisson Fort George Hotel last Wednesday, July 2, 1997.

Sadie Vernon has been an ardent supporter of Rotary over the years and, as a part of her lifetime commitment to helping the underprivileged, she has assisted Rotary Belize for the past 10 years with its annual Senior Citizens Christmas Dinner (*Amandala* July 13, 1997)

Public Recognition Ceremony
Belize Council of Churches—1997

A Public Recognition Ceremony honouring Sadie Vernon was sponsored by the Belize Council of Churches. Words of acknowledgement were presented by Bishop O. P. Martin, Roman Catholic Church; Rev. Father Leroy Flowers, President, Belize Council of Churches; Mrs. Retha McCutcheon, World Ministries of Friends United Meeting; Mrs. Sandra Francis, Principal of the Belize Continuation School; and Michael Cain, Principal, Friends Boys School.

As we remember Miss Sadie's service to the church, to the community and to us all, we remember that she is God's gift to us all! She has given herself in love to the ministry of the Christian faith! This poem reminds us of what she would say to the poor and needy:

> You have needs that I cannot meet,
>   but what I have I give you!
> You have plans I can't imagine,
>   but what I have I give you!
> I can't fulfill your fondest dreams,
>   or satisfy your dearest sadness,
> Or even comprehend your dreams,
>   but what I have I give you.
> Even speaking heart to heart,
>   the two of us seem so far apart.
> I really don't know where to start,
>   but what I have I give you.
> You have pain that is all your own
>   And hurt you carry all alone.
> You have seen grief I have never known,
>   But what I have I give you.
> Will you do the same for me?
>   For I have needs like yours you see.
> So could your word of comfort be:
>   "What I have I give you!"

Sadie Vernon High School—September 6. 1999

On September 6th, 1999, a ceremony was held to rename the Belize Continuation School "Sadie Vernon High School". In attendance were the Minister of Education, Permanent Secretary for the Ministry of Education, the faculty and entire student body of Sadie Vernon High School, family and friends of Sadie Vernon.

Introduction of Ms. Sadie Vernon

It is my distinguished privilege to introduce you to Ms. Sadie Vernon. She has been a part of the development and improvement of our Belizean society since long before some of us were born. She has been involved with the church, government, and non-governmental organizations. It seems that her main mission in life is to care and to equip the poor with skills that will only better them. Ms. Vernon is a woman to be honoured and revered.

She was born March 20th, 1918, the daughter of Elsa Agatha Maheia Vernon and Frederick Vernon. She had one sibling and his name was Frederick Vernon. She was born in Belize City and spent most of her childhood here. She left Belize in her early twenties headed for Jamaica to be a teacher. She has travelled and lived widely throughout the Caribbean, Central America and the United States. She has been an educator, nurse, counsellor, missionary and manager. She attended St. Hilda's High School. Later, she earned the Master of Ministry from Earlham School of Religion.

She has worked as the Executive Secretary with the Belize Council of Churches from 1963 until her retirement. She has given speeches all over the United States on varied topics. ...

Ms. Vernon spearheaded the birth of the Belize Continuation School. She wrote up a project for twenty girls and presented it when a group of Church Women United visited in 1963. Classes were held for girls at the YWCA building. It was a joint project between the YWCA and the Christian Social Council with Church Women United. She is a visionary.

Ms. Vernon is a highly spiritual person. She is always ready to listen and has a positive outlook on whatever challenge comes her way. One cannot help but be in awe when in her presence. She is always mannerly and has a stately demeanour. I am proud to introduce this woman, a woman beyond her time! (*Elizabeth Allen, (God-daughter to Sadie Vernon, 6th September 1999*)

Sadie Vernon High
The Temple of My Learning

I am a student.
I was born the first moment that a question
leaped from my mouth as a poor child.

I've had many dreams about many things.
And all I've ever needed is a place and someone
To develop my mind.

I am a student.
This is my school –
Sadie Vernon High—the temple of my learning.
It is a sacred place of knowledge and skills.
It is the next step from only dreaming.

Take a good look around.
This is my magnificent domain.
This is my honourable sanctuary.
The refuge, where all my profound, philosophical
Thoughts are created, manipulated and empowered.

Yes! You can find me here, bigger than the deepest
Parts of the oceans and as immeasurable as the
Greatest need in your heart!
I challenge you, lay the grounds for my upliftment!
—Renold Bolden

www.ingramcontent.com/pod-product-compliance
Lightning Source LLC
Chambersburg PA
CBHW050147170426
43197CB00011B/1995